# SURVIVAL GUIDE
# *Beginning*
# *Fly Anglers*

## Skip Morris

**Frank Amato**
**Publications**

**PORTLAND**

**SKIP MORRIS** is known to fly-fishers around the world through his 15 other fly-fishing books (*Morris & Chan on Fly Fishing Trout Lakes, Tactics for Trout, The Art of Tying the Bass Fly, Fly Tying Made Clear and Simple,* and *Western River Hatches* to name only a few) and the hundreds of magazine articles he's published in a long list of fly-fishing and outdoor magazines (*Fly Fisherman, Fly Tyer, Fly Rod & Reel, Western Outdoors, Fly Fusion,* and *Flyfishing & Tying Journal* among others). He played host on a broadcast fly-fishing TV show for three years and has appeared as a guest on various TV and radio shows. He has spoken at fly-fishing and sportsmen's events across the US and Canada and overseas. His original fly designs are tied and marketed by the Solitude Fly Company.

Skip and his wife, Carol Ann, fish and explore waters from Sweden to Maryland to Montana and many points between. They live with two battling cats on Washington State's lush Olympic Peninsula. Visit Skip's web-site: www.skip-morris-fly-tying.com

All inquiries should be addressed to:
**Frank Amato Publications, Inc.**
P.O. Box 82112 • Portland, Oregon 97282
www.amatobooks.com • (503) 653-8108

All photos (unless otherwise noted) and illustrations by Carol Ann Morris
Cover and book design by Tony Amato
All flies tied by Skip Morris
SB ISBN-13: 978-1-57188-522-7    SB ISBN-10: 1-57188-522-6    SB UPC: 0-81127-00375-4

Printed in Singapore

# Contents

*Mono Loop knot p24*

*River Trout bare bones list p49*

Acknowledgments 4

| | | |
|---|---|---|
| Chapter 1 | Equipment | 5 |
| Chapter 2 | Flies and the Creatures They Imitate | 15 |
| Chapter 3 | Knots and Rigging Up | 22 |
| Chapter 4 | Fly Casting | 27 |
| Chapter 5 | Finding Fish | 34 |
| Chapter 6 | Hooking, Playing, and Landing Fish and Such | 36 |
| Chapter 7 | Trout in Rivers | 41 |
| Chapter 8 | Largemouth Bass and Bluegills in Lakes | 52 |
| Chapter 9 | Smallmouth Bass in Rivers | 58 |
| Chapter 10 | Trout in Lakes | 64 |
| Chapter 11 | Fine Points that Matter | 71 |
| Chapter 12 | Other Fishes | 75 |
| Chapter 13 | Tying Flies | 77 |
| Chapter 14 | Safety | 78 |
| Chapter 15 | Skip's Tips | 79 |

Index 80

# Acknowledgements

On completion of each of my previous thirteen books I've been struck by the wealth of invaluable help I received along the way and by how much the book was improved by it. Well, it just happened again—right now I'm thinking of the friends and other good people who contributed so much to this book. And, to the videos. So...

I'll start by thanking those who made possible many of the photos and so much of the video by providing access, guidance, or both. To Five Rivers Lodge in Dillon, Montana for helping me and the crew figure out where, when, and how to connect with insect hatches and brown trout in those magnificent nearby rivers (and for a week's lodging and gourmet meals). To Terry and Peggy Long of Canyon Creek Ranch in Mitchell, Oregon for our time on both their lake of big trout and pond crowded with fun-size largemouth bass and peppered with hefty panfish defending their turf. To G.L. Britton of Double Spey Outfitters in Spokane, Washington who helped us find, hook, photograph, and shoot video of big rainbow trout through a long private stretch of a little spring creek winding through the dust and sagebrush of Eastern Washington desert.

My thanks to Gary Lewis, outdoor writer and host of the television show "Gary Lewis's Adventure Journal," for solid advice on where to find all sorts of fish and fishing for both the book photos and video during that long "business trip" to Central Oregon. To Jeff Perin, owner of The Fly Fisher's Place in Sisters,

Oregon, for arranging our time on Terry and Peggy's Canyon Creek Ranch.

For helping me figure out which fly patterns are popular, effective, and likely to remain easy for you to find over the next decade or two, my thanks to Randy Stetzer. And to Joel La Follette, for letting us shoot video of various wading boots and sunglasses for half a day at his Royal Treatment fly shop in West Linn, Oregon.

Thanks to my now-friend-and-fishing-pal Jeff Welker, who didn't know a tippet from a reel seat when he happily agreed to play the part of test subject—and who instinctively uncovered considerable stumbles, inconsistencies, and muddled sentences and paragraphs in my text.

For all that work shooting and editing video—as well as handling that big camera while wading rapids (and once, sloshing for shore in a deflating pontoon boat while hoisting the heavy camera in a panic above the rising water line)—my thanks to my talented friend Brian Rose. To my talented wife, Carol Ann Morris, for the care and determination she poured into every illustration and photograph. To talented (lucky me, surrounded by talented people!) Tony Amato for another artful and effective book design. Finally, to Frank Amato for putting his faith in and money and time and effort behind my eleventh book for Frank Amato Publications. (And Frank, yes, you're talented too.)

Honest, everybody, I couldn't have done this half as well without you all.

# CHAPTER 1

# Equipment

The most important thing you need to know about fly-fishing equipment (often called "tackle," especially when referring specifically to rods, reels, and fly lines) is that it does not *have* to be complicated. At their core, the fly-fisher's tools are simple: a fly on the end of fine level leader (called "tippet") attached to a tapered leader, the stout butt of the tapered leader attached to the point of a tapered line, a reel to contain the line and a rod to cast it. This is the uncluttered image to hold in your mind as you face the sometimes dizzying array of options and variations in fly-fishing equipment; just scan a catalog, online or paper, and you'll see what I mean. Take leaders—do you want knotted or pre-tapered, 9 foot or 12 foot, fluorocarbon, furled? And reels—should yours be large-arbor, multiplying, should it have rim control?

Have I got you all jumpy now? Relax. The thing is, there are straightforward, standard choices and they're *good* choices—reliable garden-variety fly equipment still catches lots of fish.

Yes, there are some details you need to know about lines, rods, reels, waders, flies, and more, but not all that many details. So as we explore fly tackle, we'll stay close to the basics and veer away from them only when it's genuinely necessary (and then, only briefly). I'll also provide suggestions and guidelines for selecting equipment that will fit you comfortably and perform admirably.

## FLY LINE

It's logical to assume that the first item of equipment you'd choose would be your rod, but that's not how it works—the line is the foundation of your fly tackle. The weight of your fly line determines how large a fly you can rocket way out there or how quietly you can set a tiny fly onto smooth water among skittish fish, how strong a wind you can cast into, all sorts of factors.

So, you figure out what kind of fishing you'll be doing, what that fishing requires, and then you select the weight of your line—and *then* you find a rod and reel to match it. But since you're brand new at this, I'll select your line for you.

A fly line is composed of a fine, tough, flexible core within a thick, supple coating. The coating tapers from thin at the front end to thicker and then runs level for quite a ways.

This coating is especially lightweight and thick on fly lines that float, slimmer and denser on lines intended to sink.

The lengths of fly lines vary somewhat, most ranging from 90 to 120 feet. Don't worry about line length.

## Lightweight Lines

The actual scale-weight of the front 30 feet of a fly line determines its number.

Line weights numbered 0, 1, 2, 3, and 4—from very light to just light—are normally for tiny to medium-size flies, short to medium-long casts, and not much wind. I can't honestly say I've ever felt the need for a line lighter than a 4 (though some seasoned anglers like 3s or lighter for their finest fishing). Weights 0, 1, and 2 are on the edge—perhaps they offer slight advantages under the most exacting circumstances, or perhaps they're really for the sort of person who yearns to take an idea to its limit.

This clear, rich spring-fed Pennsylvania stream, whose cautious trout inspect every insect and artificial fly with care and spook at a frown, is ideal for 3- and 4-weight lines that drop lightly onto its lazy currents. A 5- or 6-weight line can do the job here admirably though.

## Heavyweight Lines

Heavy line weights 8, 9, 10, and up to 15 are the brutes—for big, up to *enormous*, flies and fishes. They'll handle just about any wind a fly-fisher would dare challenge. Rods capable of pushing out these thick lines must be stiff, and consequently are the best for wrestling big fish. (Some of the heaviest-line rods are *over*stiff—a bit awkward to cast but just the thing when that 130-pound sailfish tries to empty your reel.)

The need for lines 8 and higher is uncommon—you may end up fishing them eventually, but they're no way to start out in fly-fishing.

## Middle-Weight Lines

Line weights 5, 6, and 7 are the versatile middle-weights, for the average range of flies, fish, and conditions. A 5-weight line is a medium-light line for trout fishing in both lakes and rivers, and will handle panfishes and small largemouth and smallmouth bass.

A 7-weight line is medium-heavy, for big trout, and is a solid choice for smallmouth and largemouth bass.

A 6-weight line is the *true* middle weight—I've caught difficult trout on calm water, little bluegills in the lily pads, hefty smallmouth bass, and 20-pound silver salmon on 6 weights.

Your first line should be a 6 weight (also called a "number 6" or "size-6" line).

Just about any trout fishing and most bass fishing can be handled with a 6-weight line—from dropping little dry flies lightly among drifting insects on a river to lobbing out large streamers.

## Floating, Full-Sinking, and Sink-Tip Lines

Okay, this gets tricky, so please read slowly. A "floating" (or "full-floating") line floats, end to end.

A "full-sinking" line sinks from end to end—no part of the line floats.

A "sink-tip" line sinks only through about its front 5 to 30 feet while the rest of the line floats.

For most standard fly-fishing—trout in rivers, largemouth bass and panfishes in lakes, smallmouth bass in rivers—the floating line is normally all you need.

Trout-lake fishing is another matter—it's not exactly standard fly-fishing, and really requires both a *full*-sinking line and a floating line. The full-sinker gets the fly down to deep trout and holds that fly down, even as the angler retrieves it. The floating line is mostly for surface-feeding and shallow trout. All the sinking lines I found in my research are dark colors, which is good—dark is hard for fish to see in deep water.

Sink-*tip* lines are mainly for rivers, for fishing flies that imitate substantial, active creatures such as little fishes, crayfish, and leeches. The line's tip stays down in the deeper

No problem tossing large flies for largemouth and smallmouth bass with a versatile 6-weight line, as here. For particularly big bass, heavier lines may be better. But a 6-weight can deliver in most situations.

water while the floating part of the line rides atop the shallows. Most sink-tips are dark through the sinking section and pale through the rest of the line.

Both full-sinking and sink-tip lines sink at various rates, and each rate is described as a "type" followed by a Roman numeral. Low-number lines sink slowly—a type I seems almost to hover. High-number lines sink fast—a type IV line cuts quickly through the water to head down with purpose. (All sorts of designations are used for lines that sink really quickly, such as "lead core" and "300 grain," but that's not important now.)

Your first fly line should be a floating line, in a light color you can see easily—yellow, orange, cream...

Fly-line shorthand—the "WF" means "weight forward," the "6" means "6 weight," and the "F" means "floating": a weight-forward, 6-weight, floating fly line.

## Taper

Fly lines come in two standard tapers:

      (1.) weight forward

      (2.) double taper

All sinking lines—both full-sinking and sink-tip—are weight-forward tapers. Full-floating lines can be double taper or weight forward. The double-taper floating line has its followers, but the standard is the weight-forward taper—your first fly line should be a weight-forward taper.

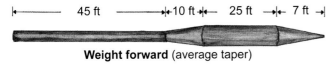

**Weight forward** (average taper)

The weight-forward line is tapered from thin in the front, then thick for a bit, then tapered to thin again, remaining thin to the end.

**Double taper** (average taper)

The double-taper line is thick and level throughout its long center, and tapered on the ends.

## JUST THE BASICS

### Now you know exactly which fly line to buy:

weight-forward taper, 6-weight, floating (in yellow, orange...).

    The box for this line would be marked "WF-6-F". (Exceptions: if you start your fly-fishing on trout lakes, you'll also buy a weight-forward, 6-weight, type III, full-sinking line, in a dark color. If you start fly-fishing on smallmouth bass rivers you'll eventually want your second line to be a 6-weight with a type-III sinking tip of 10 to 15 feet, designated as "WF 6 F/S type III," the very line you'll want, after considerable experience with dry-fly and nymph fishing, for streamers in trout rivers.)

## FLY ROD

I've heard it said that the fly-fisher's rod is his or her most personal item of equipment, and I agree. Just as most people know whether they like or dislike oysters after one bite, a seasoned fly-fisher will know whether an unfamiliar fly rod is a good fit after making just a few casts with it. The length, stiffness, and weight of a particular rod combined with the *way* it flexes, and numerous lesser factors, all instill that rod with a particular character, often called its "feel," and that character must suit the character of the angler if the two are going to make a good team. I designed fly rods as a profession for ten years; trust me—rod-feel matters.

A major element of rod-feel is "action," how a rod flexes. A rod's "power," its *overall* stiffness, is also important. And a rod's length and corresponding line-weight are critical factors in selecting the right fly rod for your fishing.

    Truth is, the feel, action, power, and other genuinely important aspects of a fly rod are hard to nail down. You won't get a lot of help with this from catalogs or web-sites—but you will below.

## Parts of a Fly Rod

The heart of a modern graphite fly rod is its long, hollow shafts joined together by one or more "ferrules," rigid, overlapping joints that allow the rod's sections to be pulled apart for storage. The rod-shafts are fitted with these standard components: a "reel seat," a screw-locking assembly to hold the reel; a "handle" or "grip" of cork (occasionally of some synthetic material); "guides," coils of wire that direct the line, mounted at intervals; and a "tip-top," the final guide mounted on the rod's fine point. Rods for really big fish may include a "fighting butt," a rigid extension below the reel seat with a large, rounded end. *Vice & Chrome*

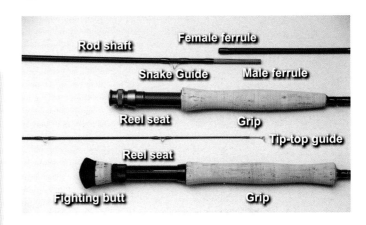

## Line Weight

A fly rod is designed to handle a specific line weight. So if the rod is, say, eight-feet six-inches long and designed for a 6-weight line, something like this will be printed on the rod-shaft just above the grip:

$$6 \text{ wt} \quad 8'6''$$

Or it might say "8 foot 6 inch No. 6" or such.

    Some rods are rated for two line-weights. There are theories about this. One theory: the lower-number line-weight is for double-taper lines and the higher one for weight-forward. Another theory: one line-weight for distance casting the other for standard range. And so on. Maybe, but I think it all goes back to personal taste—I think the two line-weights printed on some rods really say, "Try these lines and see which you like best." This does make matching rods and lines a little tricky, but here's a simple solution: if a rod is rated for two lines, consider it a rod for the *heavier* of the two lines. So a "5-6 weight" rod is really a 6-weight rod.

    Since you'll get a 6-weight line, your first rod should be designated for a versatile 6-weight line (or, again "5 or 6").

## Length

Guidelines for fly-rod length keep changing. The standard length when I was a kid was around 7 1/2 feet—that's considered a truly short rod now.

My advice: if you're an adult of at least average height, get a rod around 9 feet long (not under 8 1/2 feet). If you're a boy or girl or a small woman you'll probably do best with a rod 8 to 8 1/2 feet long. (Following this logic, for a really young kid or especially small woman, an 8-foot rod.) If you possibly can, try casting various rods at a fly shop to see what fits.

Rod length is pretty personal—if you're a 6-foot-4-inch-tall man who likes an 8-foot rod, you should have one. And if you're a small woman who likes a 9 1/2-foot rod, be my guest. But such tastes normally develop over years.

So choose the length of your first rod by the guidelines of the second paragraph above.

## Sections

Most fly rods were made in two sections until around the 1990s—before then, four-section (or "four-piece") rods were marketed mainly for anglers who hiked long distances to fish. Now the four-section rod is about as common as the two-section. Today's ferrules, made simply of overlapping rod-sections, are lightweight and have very little effect on a rod's weight, action, and feel. And four-section rods fit into short cases that really are a blessing for hiking, car travel, and air travel (although four-section rods cost more than two-section rods). There are three- and five- and even six-section rods; later you may prefer one of these, but it's hard to beat a four-section rod for a blend of performance and convenience.

Your rod should be four sections or two sections (prefer a four-section rod if you can afford it).

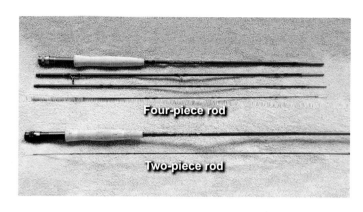

Four-piece rod

Two-piece rod

## Rod Action

Basically, "action" is the specific way a rod bends as it's cast. This bend strongly influences the width of the casting loops in the line, the timing of casts, how easily the rod makes a short cast or a long cast, and more. Rod action *is* a big deal.

Here are the basic rod actions:

*Slow action:* the lower half, the "butt section," of the rod really flexes. A slow-action rod seems to lag behind your casting stroke, which some experienced fly-fishers prefer.

*Fast action:* the butt section of the rod is stiff, with most of the flexing going on well up the rod, towards its tip. A fast-action rod doesn't hesitate at all, but springs to life as soon as the cast begins. As with slow-action rods, fast-action rods suit some fly-fishers perfectly. With the fastest rods you'll tend to rush your casting stroke just keep up with the rod.

*Moderate action:* the butt section does some flexing, but not a lot. The moderate-action rod responds promptly to your casting stroke, but neither aggressively like a fast-action rod nor lazily like a slow-action rod. Moderate-action rods are the most versatile and the easiest to cast.

## ROD ACTION

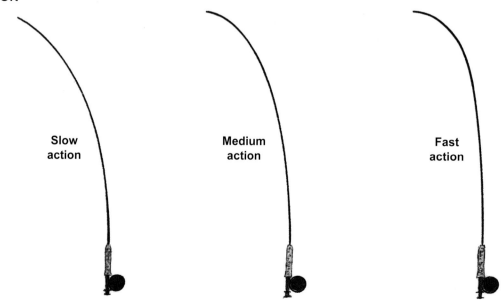

Slow action

Medium action

Fast action

Don't even try to bend rods or watch how a rod flexes as you cast it—this is a tricky way to determine rod action even for a professional rod designer. Just feel how the rod responds—if it seems to resist and respond slowly, it's action is slow; if it responds immediately and feels stiff, its action is fast. Often, the manufacturer's web-site or brochure, or the pamphlet that comes with the rod, will describe the rod's action.

You'll eventually develop a preference for a certain rod action—it's, again, a really personal issue for experienced casters. But for now, get a rod with an action you'll never really outgrow.

Your first rod should have moderate (to slightly fast) action.

## Power

"Power" in a fly rod simply refers to the stiffness of the rod in relation to the weight of the line. In other words, in relation to how much the line works, "loads," the rod. A powerful rod won't seem to flex much until you make a long cast because a lot of line (say, 70 feet) weighs much more than a moderate length of line (30 feet, for example). A rod with low power will feel just right on a short cast but may seem to collapse on a long cast.

A rod with medium power will feel good casting from short to long, making it very versatile.

It's easy to confuse rod power with rod action, but just think of it this way: "Action" is about the shape of the bend in a rod as it's cast, while "power" is about a rod's overall stiffness (in relation to a specific line weight).

You want your first rod to be about medium in power.

To find a medium-power rod, check what the manufacturer says in its promotional literature (online or in print) about a particular model, and try casting the rod at a fly shop to see if it feels overly stiff on a short cast (say, 15 feet of line out) or just seems to give out on a long cast (about 60 feet of line out, at least 50 feet). If the rod handles both short and long casts well, it's power is moderate (which is what you want...remember?). One problem: you may not have a way to learn to cast before buying a rod. If so, buy a rod marketed as having middle-range action and power.

## Material

This is easy. From the 1950s until the mid 1970s you had two choices in fly-rod materials: split bamboo and tubular fiberglass. Bamboo was expensive and the heavier and least durable of the two, but afficionados loved it. They still do, and a fine bamboo rod is elegance in craftsmanship with an earthy feel that can get into your bones. But "glass" made some excellent rods whose prices were often very attractive. Then came graphite rods in the 70s and through the 80s they simply took over. Graphite is still the standard fly-rod material—and less expensive than ever.

Your first fly rod should be made of tubular graphite.

## Case and Bag

Here's how it works: get a rod case, protect the rod; no case, break the rod. Rods get beaten up or broken quickly when they're transported and stored without a case. A rod case is simply a tube with a removable top. You slip the rod into a cloth bag, and then slip the rod and bag into the case.

Some rods come with a bag built into the case, most come with a separate bag and case. Regardless, make sure you have a bag and case for your rod, and use them.

---

## JUST THE BASICS

**Now you know which fly rod to buy:**

**Line:** 6-weight line. (If the rod is designated for two lines, prefer "5/6" over "6/7")

**Length:** 9 feet (for most, but reread the section on rod length)

**Sections:** 4 preferred but 2 is fine

**Action:** moderate to slightly fast action

**Power:** medium power

**Material:** graphite

**Fighting butt:** no fighting butt (no problem, though, if the rod has one)

**Bag and Case:** you need a rod bag and rod case, or you'll soon own a broken rod.

Consider visiting fly-fishing shops and out-door-sports stores both to cast various rods and to get the advice of the salespeople, or call a mail-order fly-fishing supply house and talk with the staff. After a little shopping around and asking questions, you'll probably feel comfortable selecting a rod.

Consider rods—and complete combos of rod, reel, and line—marketed specifically for beginners. Such rods are usually a good choice for starting out and quite affordable.

---

## REEL

A standard "single-action" fly reel (no gears or springs or such) is composed of a "frame" (the housing that contains the spool), a "spool" (which holds line and rotates within the frame), a "foot" (which mounts in the rod's reel seat), a handle (for turning the spool), and a drag (usually adjustable, to resist the runs of large fish).

A fly reel's duties are simple: store the line, take in unnecessary line, give line when needed, and put pressure on a big fish. But the reel must perform its duties well or you'll come to hate the sight of it. A reel with too much space between the rim of the spool and the frame will catch the line and jam—an excellent way to lose that trophy fish or just go insane. And there are plenty of other ways a fly reel can fail: the drag dies; the spool falls out, seizes up, goes loose; perhaps the whole reel just comes off its foot and thumps to the dust at your feet...

So, you need a single-action fly reel, not necessarily expensive but reliable. But don't shop for a reel yet...

## Backing

A fly line is not connected directly to a reel, but to a considerable length of "backing," fine braided twine, and the backing is attached to the reel's spool. This backing keeps a big fish from running out all your fly line and then breaking free—instead, the fish just keeps running as the backing follows the line out (and the reel's drag resists).

So, buy a fly reel with the capacity to hold your WF-6-F fly line and 50 to 100 yards of 20-pound-test braided fly-line backing. (Prefer 100 yards for trout-lake fishing).

## Fly Reel Options

### PARTS OF A FLY REEL

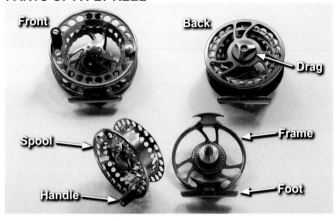

Many fly reels now have "rim control," the rim of the spool is exposed so the angler can lightly press the palm of the hand against it when the drag needs help: "palming" the reel. This is a useful but certainly not critical feature.

A "large-arbor" reel has a wide core in its spool, to help keep the fly line from taking a curl and to even out the drag's resistance. Large-arbor reels are bigger than reels with standard spools. I along with most fly-fishers have come to prefer large-arbor reels. But reels with standard spools work fine—I fished them successfully for decades.

Most fly reels take interchangeable spools, and this really is a blessing—spools, each with a different sort of line, can be quickly switched as needed. A spool costs about half what a reel costs, saving you money, and is lighter than a reel, making it convenient to carry additional lines on the water.

Always—*always!*—put the peel-off label (that comes with a fly line) on the spool holding the line. Always...

### JUST THE BASICS

**Now you know which fly reel to buy:**

**Design:** single action

**Capacity:** WF 6 floating line and backing (guidelines for backing are on this page)

**Interchangeable spools:** you want a reel with this option, and one extra spool for trout lakes. Possibly, one extra spool for smallmouth and trout rivers.

## TAPERED LEADER

To the tip-end of a fly line is normally attached a "tapered leader," a monofilament strand, tapered from thick at its butt-end to fine at its point. If the thick fly line were connected directly to the fly, no sane fish would be fooled, so the clear leader (and tippet, which comes next) separate line and fly.

Tapered leaders range from short (around 6 feet long and shorter) to long (around 8 feet long and longer, up to 12 feet and beyond).

The thickness of the point of a leader (which is described with "X." I'll explain next) determines its breaking strain.

There are all sorts of tapered-leader variations—"knotted" leaders built of level monofilament sections tied together, "furled" leaders of fine woven monofilament strands, and others. For now, forget all those.

So you need at least two standard tapered "knotless" leaders (four for trout lakes) to start fly-fishing. The specifics on these leaders will depend on what fish and water you choose for beginning your career as a fly-fisher (we'll get to that).

## TIPPET

On the point of a tapered fly leader you normally knot on two to three feet of "tippet," fine level monofilament. The tippet, because it's untapered, tends to land in coils on the water, which helps keep shifting currents from unnaturally dragging a dry fly (and other flies). Tippet also helps a nymph or other underwater fly sink because tippet is slimmer than tapered leader. And its cheaper to cut off some tippet when you change flies than to trim back and shorten the life of an expensive tapered leader.

There is standard tippet, which works fine. "Fluorocarbon" tippet, though expensive, is less visible in water than standard tippet—but it sinks, making it a problem for floating flies. Start with standard tippet.

Tippet is sized by its diameter. Tapered leaders are sized by the diameter of their fine points. This diameter is given an "X" rating. It's all very odd, but that's how it's long been done. Here's how it works: the higher the number in front of the "X," the finer the tippet. So a 7X tippet is very fine and a 2X is much thicker and stronger. After OX, the designation goes 01X, 02X, and heavier and heavier, or the "X" just goes away and the breaking point in pounds is given.

Normally the tippet is one or two sizes (Xs) smaller than the size of the point of the leader (for example: 3X tippet with a 2X or 1X leader).

The tippet you want will be determined by the kind of fishing you choose to start out with. You'll soon be presented with four types of fishing—pick one, and then just follow the tippet recommendations that go with it.

As a tippet grows shorter with each fly you cut off and each new fly you tie on, it eventually becomes too short, perhaps two thirds of its original length—that's when you tie on a whole new length of tippet. Usually, the tapered leader will become frayed and coiled and knotted before it's been cut too short for more tippet. Replace your leader if it is knotted (and if you can't take out the knots) or frayed or stubbornly coiled...or if its tip is now way thicker than the tippet you need to attach to it.

## FLIES

There are—*literally*—tens of thousands of established fly-designs. Actually, you need only a few reliable flies for most of your fishing in most places (a list of flies is provided in each of the four chapters on specific types of fishing). But the topic of flies deserves its own chapter, and gets it: chapter 2: "Flies and the Creatures They Imitate."

## WADERS AND SUCH

Most fly-fishing is practiced on rivers, and for fishing rivers—except during hot summer days in certain places—you'll need "waders," sort of waterproof overalls with waterproof feet (or with waterproof boots attached) to keep you dry and warm. "Wading boots" go on over the wader-feet of "stockingfoot" (bootless) waders and provide a good grip on a riverbed. A "wading belt" keeps the waders gathered for comfort and adds safety if you fall in. And some kind of "wading staff" helps you balance as you wade—a serious safety factor.

That's the list of equipment for wading. Here are some considerations.

Air passes through "breathable" waders while water cannot, which lets perspiration evaporate to avoid sweat-soaked legs and feet at the end of the day. But breathable waders are more expensive than old-fashioned waders that trap air. Old-fashioned waders served me honorably for decades.

"Stockingfoot" waders, which have soft feet of fabric or neoprene, are now the norm, and require wading boots to go over them—this combination is best for an active day's wading. "Bootfoot" waders come with waterproof boots attached, and they're quicker to enter and exit than stockingfoot waders and fine when you're mostly just standing to wade.

Wading boots needn't be rigid, but should provide some support so your feet don't turn on rocks to injure your ankles. Wading boots and bootfoot waders come with textured soles to grip a riverbed, but "studded" soles, peppered with little metal peaks, provide serious traction. Studded soles damage boats, so if you plan on drifting a river, forget studs.

Wading belts are fairly inexpensive, and you need one.

Wading staffs cost a bit, but an old ski pole with the basket cut off functions well, as does a stout stick. Special collapsible wading staffs that tuck into a holster are great, though expensive. A wading staff of some kind is wise in rivers.

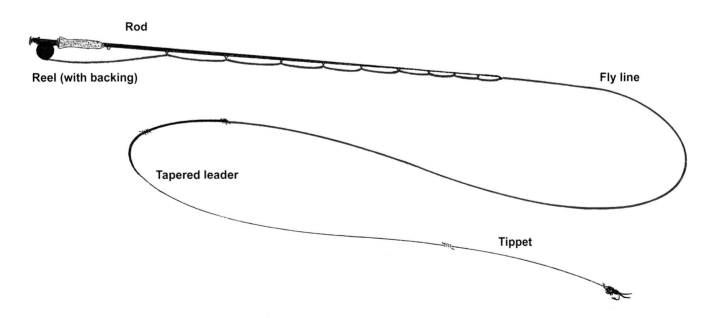

Rod

Reel (with backing)

Fly line

Tapered leader

Tippet

## BOATS AND FLOAT TUBES

If you're going to fish lakes and reservoirs, you'll need some kind of watercraft—it's typically close to impossible to fly-fish effectively on standing water without one. The standard watercraft for fishing lakes is a boat. For smaller lakes, a rowboat will serve you well.

Various inflatable watercraft have really caught on for fly fishing lakes, specifically the "float tube," an air-filled doughnut-shaped bladder with a cover that includes a seat, backrest, and compartments for gear; the "V-boat," which is essentially a float tube open in front for easy entry and exit; and the "pontoon boat" or "kick boat," a frame and seat and the rest, mounted between two inflatable pontoons. Float tubes and V-boats are powered by swim fins. Kick boats are normally powered by swim fins or oars. Never go out in a craft that dangles your feet in the water where there are water snakes, alligators, or the like.

So you need to buy swim fins for a float tube or V-boat or kick boat (although some pontoon boats are really designed to be rowed, and these usually come with oars), and waders.

Unless you have a boat designed for rivers, do not take that boat out on a river (and never take any boat out on a river unless you *really* know what you're doing). *Never* go out on a river in a float tube or V-boat. Go out on a river in a pontoon boat only if you're sure it's a pontoon boat *made* for rivers and, again, know your stuff.

Boat

In a boat, you'll need to bring a life vest or other Coast Guard-approved floatation device. (See chapter 14, "Safety" for more on handling a boat, float tube, V-boat, or kick boat safely.)

## GADGETS AND TRAPPINGS

You'll soon read four chapters that each prepare you for a different kind of fly-fishing. Once you've chosen the kind of fishing you'll start out with, the corresponding chapter will tell you which items you'll need from the list below.

*Glasses: Polarized* sunglasses, either prescription or over-the-counter, let you see through the glare and beneath the surface of water—a *real* advantage, particularly where water is clear. But, *always* wear glasses of some kind whenever you cast a fly or are even near someone casting a fly. I'll spare you the fly-in-the-eye stories, but glasses will save you from creating such a story of your own.

Clear safety glasses from a hardware store (or your own clear prescription glasses) beat sunglasses for evening and early morning fishing.

*Sunscreen:* That sun we fish under all day can be a health risk. A good sunscreen, applied liberally and often, reduces that risk.

*Vest:* A fly-fishing vest with its multitude of pockets holds all sorts of things you need (flies, leaders, tippet, clippers, extra reels, lunch, water...) in an organized, handy way. But hip and chest packs have earned devoted followings.

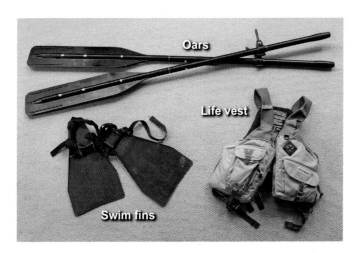

Oars

Life vest

Swim fins

Kick boat (pontoon boat)

Chest pack

Vest

Sunglasses

Fly box

Clear glasses

Fly box

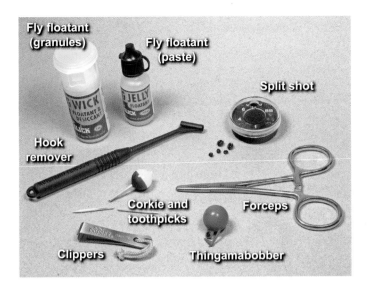

Fly floatant (granules)
Fly floatant (paste)
Split shot
Hook remover
Corkie and toothpicks
Forceps
Clippers
Thingamabobber

**Net:** Not required, but a blessing when fishing for trout in a river or lake.

**Hook Hone:** For sharpening fly-hooks. Handy, but you can wait to get one. A smooth river stone can substitute.

**Strike Indicator:** For fishing nymphs in trout rivers and for a special technique in trout lakes. You'll need a few if you're going to fish trout rivers or trout lakes. There are yarn and putty indicators and others—and they all work and all have believers. The two I currently prefer are the "corkie," a brightly painted cork ball with a hole in the center and the Thingamabobber, a sort of tiny balloon with a plastic peg.

**First-aid Kit:** You'd be wise to pack a small one along.

## CLOTHING

To a fly-fisher, clothing is mostly about staying warm or cool, dry, and protected from the sun.

Breathable rain jacket
Wide-brim hat
Lightweight long-sleeve shirt
Lightweight and heavy fingerless gloves
Heavy wading socks

**Fly Box:** Boxes with open compartments hold lots of flies but can make finding a particular fly difficult. Boxes in which the flies are stuck in foam or pushed into slits in foam hold fewer flies, but display them all neatly. Buy your flies first, and then select a box that suits their size and shape.

**Clippers:** These are for cutting leader and tippet. You'll use them regularly. The ones made specifically for fly-fishers are the lightest and smallest, but fingernail clippers work.

**Floatant:** A paste or liquid or granules you apply to a floating fly to increase its buoyancy. Start with paste.

**Weight:** You add this to your tippet to help carry a fly down. Such weight comes as "split shot," tiny and round (the size varies) that crimps on; "lead putty," pliable weight you form and press on, and others. Nontoxic lead substitutes are best for water and fish and you. Start with split shot.

**Hook Remover:** Practically a must for trout and panfishes, though still helpful with bass even though you can normally reach down into their wide mouths to remove your large fly. Forceps are the reliable standard hook removers (I clamp them onto my vest), but some fly-fishers prefer other styles.

**Fly Patch or Dryer:** A patch of wool or ventilated container pinned to your vest, to hold your used flies as they dry, before you put them away in your fly boxes—damp flies in fly boxes wind up on rusted hooks.

**Hat:** Its brim shades your polarized sunglass so they can work effectively and shades your skin to avoid sunburn and worse. You need a hat with a brim, according to the American Cancer Society, "wide enough to shade face, ears, and neck..."

If you plan to fish in chilly weather—or if there's any chance you'll end up fishing in such weather despite your plans—you'll be glad to have a second, warm, insulated hat that covers your ears and straps under your chin.

**Shirts and Jackets:** A fishing shirt should cover your arms and chest and at least some of your neck—this, along with sunscreen, is critical for long days outdoors. Shirts and jackets must also provide warmth in cold weather, so wear mostly lightweight fabrics and *layer* them. This allows you to take off or put on layers to adjust for the weather.

Bringing a waterproof raincoat's always a good idea—it can protect you from wind and rain both.

**Gloves:** Fingerless gloves of lightweight UV-resistant fabric are standard now to protect fly-fishers' hands from sunshine. Heavy fingerless gloves of thick wool or synthetic fabric do the same while warming your hands when the air is frigid.

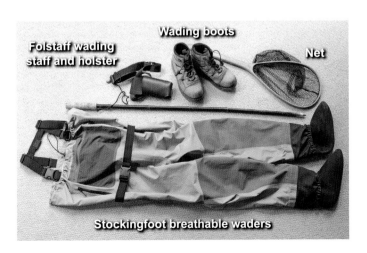

Folstaff wading staff and holster
Wading boots
Net
Stockingfoot breathable waders

# CARING FOR YOUR TACKLE

With a little knowledge and care you can make your tackle last long. I'll provide the knowledge; the care is your department.

First, remember to store *all* your gear where sunshine can't reach it—ultraviolet rays will quickly break down waders, lines, leaders, flies...

*Rod:* Never—*never*—put your rod away wet or in a wet rod bag or a wet rod case; water vapor will damage the finish on the rod and reel seat and guide windings, perhaps weaken the glue holding on the reel seat—really. Just don't do it.

Things that close—house doors, car doors and trunks—love to break fly rods. Watch out...

Now and then wipe down your rod, reel seat, guides, and all with a soft dry cloth, especially the guides—dirty guides really wear on a fly line.

Never drop your rod on the ground, of course. But also be careful how and where you set it, which means *gently* on hard surfaces (never on *rough* hard surfaces) and not precariously upright so that it might tip over. If you set the rod atop your car, don't drive off while it's still up there...happens all the time.

*Reel:* Keep your reel oiled (or greased, whichever the manufacturer recommends). Do not set your reel down in silt or sand, because these will wear quickly on the bearings and, in fact, the rest of the spool and frame. If you get sand or silt in the reel, remove the spool and wash everything out. If necessary, wipe out the lubricant and then add more.

Never set your reel on a rough surface, whether that reel is on your rod or not. Be careful not to drop your reel, of course; if you bend the frame, the reel may be ruined.

*Fly Line:* A fly line is expensive compared with most fishing lines, so you have to take its care seriously. Wipe the length of your line with a soft clean cloth whenever the line seems even a little dirty or gritty. You can then wipe on a thin coating of fly-line dressing (inexpensive, and there are always a few brands around) if you like; dressing will protect the line and make it slick. Otherwise, avoid stepping on the line or getting it dirty, and keep it away from anything that might cut, scrape, or abrade the line's soft coating. Remember also that a dirty line will quickly wear out the guides on your rod.

Try not to wind the line tightly on the reel before putting the reel away between fishing days or trips, as this will put tight coils in the line, inviting it to tangle.

*Waders:* After fishing, dry your waders by turning them inside-out, letting the insides dry; then turning them outside-out to finish drying.

*Wading Boots:* Let them dry before storing them, or store them openly so they can continue drying. If the felted soles of your wading boots wear thin or come loose, contact the manufacturer. Your fly shop can possibly replace the soles or recommend someone who can.

*Saltwater Note:* Though none of the types of fishing I'll describe in detail involve salt water, some types do, so... Saltwater is tough on flies and tackle. You'll need to thoroughly rinse your rods, reels, and flies in fresh water and let them dry at the end of each saltwater fishing day.

## JUST THE BASICS

**So, here is a primary list of the stuff you'll need in order to start fly-fishing:**

**Fly line:** one, weight forward, 6-weight, floating, pale. (I'll soon describe four kinds of fishing, each with its own chapter, and when you've decided which kind of fishing you'll start with, check its corresponding chapter's recommendations—then you may want a second fly line)

**Fly rod:** one (for length, see "Length" earlier in this chapter under "Fly Rod"), for a 6-weight line, moderate (or slightly fast) action, moderate power, 4 piece preferred but 2 piece is fine, graphite, with a case and bag

**Fly reel:** one, single action, capacity for 50 to 100 yards of backing and a WF6 floating line, interchangeable-spool option much preferred (in fact, you may *need* a second spool for a second line—check this in the chapter on the fishing you'll start with)

**Tapered leader and tippet:** see the chapter on the specific kind of fishing you start with

**Flies:** see the chapter on the specific kind of fishing you start with

**Glasses:** always wear them when fishing

**Sunscreen:** always wear it when fishing (unless the sun's down)

**Gadgets and trappings:** clippers, floatant, strike indicators...no room here. Reread the section titled "Gadgets and Trappings" earlier in this chapter

**Required clothing:** hat with brim, long-sleeve shirt, gloves

For trout in rivers or smallmouth bass in rivers, add one pair of waders, one pair of wading boots, and one wading staff.

For largemouth bass and panfishes in lakes or reservoirs, add one watercraft (with waders and fins if required) and one life vest (even with a float tube, if you sense the need for the added safety, or your state requires it).

For trout in lakes, add one net, one watercraft (with waders and fins if required), one life vest (even with a float tube, if you want the additional safety, or if one is required in your state), two anchors for a boat, one for a float tube.

# CHAPTER 2

# Flies and the Creatures They Imitate

Casting and wading and reading water and, in fact, most of what we fly-fishers do are really just about getting a fly in front of a fish. But all that's for nothing if that fly fails to interest the fish.

Coming up with a fly that interests the fish is normally just a modest challenge. Most of the time, most of the fish we seek are pretty open-minded—they have to be. The food available to them is often a mix. For a trout in a river, this mix could be a curled-up stonefly nymph drifting near, then a grasshopper kicking helplessly on the surface of the water, and then a baby rainbow trout swept by an errant current into chasing range. A largemouth bass in a lake might snap down a frog swimming out a little too deep for its own good, followed by a fat black leech out hunting midge pupae. If these fish keep their options consistently narrowed to one particular food, that trout might grow very hungry before the next stonefly nymph comes along and that bass might starve if he's set on leeches and the lake contains relatively few. But they're not about to make that mistake.

Still, even when you face fish that are open to a range of possible food sources, a little knowledge about flies can make a huge difference in your success. And by understanding flies, you'll know which big nymph will get down to where a big trout is willing to eat it but unwilling to rise from the river bed. You'll understand which sparse dry flies make sense in rich slow streams and which are designed to stay afloat in churning, choppy rivers. It will also improve your fishing to understand the things flies imitate; we'll look at that first.

## CREATURES TROUT EAT IN RIVERS

We begin with the major insects of trout rivers. There are other insects and creatures that in a particular river or at a particular time will capture the attention of the trout, but the insects that follow will provide the action at least 90 percent of the time (maybe even 96 percent).

### Mayflies

With stout thoraxes and slender tapered abdomens arching gracefully upwards to long, fine widespread tails, with parted wings standing erect like two soft and filmy triangles, mayflies have long reigned in the estimation of fly-fishers as the royalty of aquatic insects. But it's not just their elegance that set mayflies on that throne; most mayflies do their hatching sedately out in the open—perfect opportunity for trout and angler alike.

A mayfly lives most of its life as a "nymph," six-legged and wingless, underwater. Most mayflies live in rivers, but a few live in lakes and other standing water.

**STAGES OF THE MAYFLY**

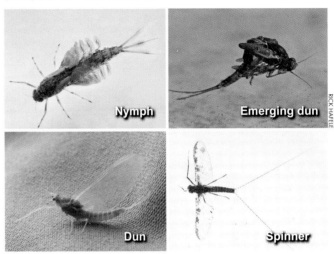

When a mayfly nymph is ripe to hatch, it swims upwards to the surface (a very few crawl from the water onto land). There, it squirms from its loosened "shuck," its underwater skin (a few kinds escape the shuck just short of the surface). Free of its shuck, the freshly hatched mayfly stands on the water resting, and drying its new wings a little while—it is now called a "dun"—and then it flies off. From under a half hour up to two days later it mates, and then fully matures to a "spinner." The female spinner flits back to the water to drop her fertilized eggs, and then lies dying on the surface as a pushover for trout. The male spinners don't normally return to the water.

There are many varieties of mayflies that are important on North American rivers and lakes, ranging from the tiny black-and-white *Tricorythodes*, or Trico, to the hulking yellow *Hexagenia*, or Hex.

Most mayfly hatches come in spring through fall, a few in winter.

### Caddisflies

The moth-like caddisfly waited a long time to get some respect. Then, in 1977, Larry Solomon and Eric Leiser turned the spotlight away from the mayfly and onto the caddisfly with their new book *The Caddis and the Angler*. Caddis deserve the attention—they're common in trout rivers and trout lakes across North America, and in Europe and beyond.

The life of all caddisflies passes through three stages. The first and by far longest stage is as a worm-like "larva," which lives in fixed shelter or moves about

## STAGES OF THE CADDISFLY

openly in a protective case it constructs. The larva turns into a "pupa," it's short second stage. The pupa vigorously strokes its long legs to ascend to the water's surface and, once there, throws off its shuck to rest quietly or scramble over the water as an "adult"; some caddis just pop right out and fly off immediately on their new wings. Adult caddis females return to the water to release their fertilized eggs.

Most caddisflies emerge from their shucks in open water, giving the trout a good shot at the pupae there, and some opportunity to catch the winged adults. (A few caddisfly types swim to shore to emerge.)

There are huge caddisflies such as the western October Caddis, medium-size ones, and on down to tiny ones some fly-fishers call "microcaddis." The long period of spring through summer and into fall is all caddis-hatching time.

## Stoneflies

Stoneflies were named for their habit of living under stones in quick currents—there are no stoneflies in lakes or any other standing water. The stonefly's life passes through only two main stages: nymph and adult. It lives most of its life as a nymph, something like a mayfly nymph, but stouter and with not one but three wing-cases up its back. At hatch time, the nymph creeps shoreward along the riverbed and finally climbs out of the water to emerge from its shuck and unfold, flex, and dry its new wings. A female will fly out over or onto the river to

## STAGES OF THE STONEFLY

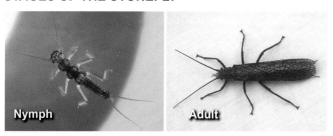

release her fertilized eggs—but males and females alike scramble around riverbank brush and grasses and tend to tumble onto the water.

Stoneflies range from the huge and celebrated western Salmonfly to the loose category of little pale stoneflies called the Yellow Sallies.

An imitation of a stonefly nymph fished freely down along a river bed is always promising, but is best just before and during the first days of a stonefly hatch. Dry-fly imitations of adults are usually fished not far out to up against the banks where the insects scamper and mate and fall into the water. But a dry fly can be good anywhere when the females are returning to the water to lay eggs.

Most stoneflies hatch in spring and summer, a few in fall and winter.

## Midges

Oddly, midges are always tiny in rivers yet much larger in lakes. The midge is a close relative of the mosquito and looks about like one, but lacks the mosquito's blood-sucking habit. A midge lives most of its life as a larva, wriggles inefficiently toward the water's surface as a pupa, and hatches as a winged adult. Normally, you fish midge-pupa, -emerger, and -adult imitations only during midge hatches, but sometimes an imitation larva will move a sullen trout in a river.

Midges hatch year round, but tend to interest trout most during the cool and cold months when few other insects are active.

## STAGES OF THE MIDGE

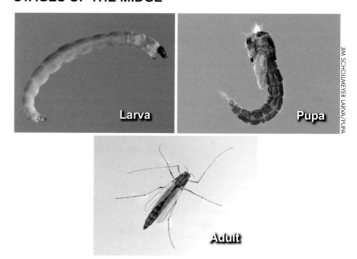

## Terrestrials

To the fly-fisher, the term "terrestrial" refers to an insect that lives on land but winds up on water. The main terrestrials are grasshoppers, ants (both wingless and winged), beetles, and cicadas, but there are others. Terrestrial insects normally fall in close to the banks, so imitations are typically presented there. Summer through early fall is terrestrial time.

## TERRESTRIALS

Beetle

Flying ant

Grasshopper

Ant

## Additional lake insects and other creatures

Lakes, like rivers, offer certain mayfly and caddis species and lots of *big* midges, which lake fishers call "Chironomids." A Chironomid hides in silt as a larva. It matures to a pupa and wriggles slowly to the surface of the water—the pupa is the most important stage to both trout and fly-fishers. At the surface the pupa escapes its shuck, flies away, and, if it's a female, later returns to the water to release her eggs.

Some insects and creatures, however, are nearly exclusive to lakes. These include the "damselfly," a long nymph that swims, often in huge numbers, toward shore to climb out on a reed, shed its shuck, and fly daintily off; the "dragonfly," a hulking brute of a nymph that crawls out of the water to emerge from its shuck as a hulking adult with remarkable flying skills; the "scud," a shrimp-like little crustacean that putters around water-weeds and fattens trout; and the "leech," a big, squishy, worm-like and almost featureless hunk of ugly trout-feed that swims something like a snake's winding movments turned upright.

## LAKE INSECTS AND CREATURES

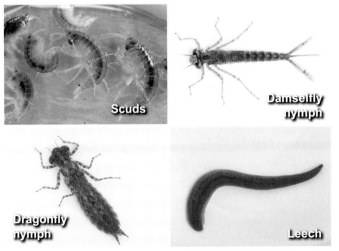

Scuds

Damselfly nymph

Dragonfly nymph

Leech

Mayflies, caddis, and Chironomids are important in spring through fall. Damselflies, spring-summer. Dragonflies, scuds, leeches, year round.

## Fishes—not just for trout

Nearly all fish eat fish. Trout eat shiners, sculpin, baby trout... Smallmouth bass eat shiners, sculpin, baby small-mouth... Largemouth bass eat shad, small bluegill, baby largemouth... Saltwater fishes around the world eat herring, anchovies, toadfish, their own babies... (Notice the theme? Baby sport-fish deal with serious family issues.)

Imitations, called streamers, are made to swim like the fishes they mimic on floating or sinking or sink-tip lines.

## SMALL FISHES

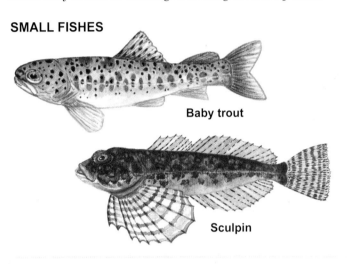

Baby trout

Sculpin

## JUST THE BASICS

**Here's a rundown of the insects and creatures on which trout and some other freshwater fishes feed:**

**Mayflies:** nymph, dun, spinner stages, in rivers and lakes

**Caddisflies:** larva, pupa, adult stages, in rivers and lakes

**Stoneflies:** nymph, adult, in rivers only

**Midges:** larva, pupa, adult, rivers and lakes

**Terrestrials:** live on land, grasshoppers, ants, beetles, cicadas

**Lake insects:** damselflies, dragonflies, Chironomids (large midges), scuds, leeches

**Fishes:** baby trout, baby bass, shiners, gobies—there are many

**Other creatures:** crayfish, adult dragonflies, and more

## Creatures bass eat

While it's true that big trout sometimes eat crayfish and even adult dragonflies, these food-types mainly interest both kinds of bass—smallmouth bass live among and relish crayfish; largemouth bass will leap for dragonflies and slam down the occasional frog. However, smallmouth bass, more than largemouth, do eat considerable quantities of the insects I've described as trout food.

Really, almost anything alive that fits into a fish's mouth is potential food for that fish. I've seen freshwater fish go after spiders, bees, and Doritos.

## FLIES

The great news about fly designs, called "fly patterns" or "fly dressings," is that although there are thousands of them out there in common use, you can go fishing with a real shot at success with just a few. The reason you can normally do well with only a few flies is, in part, thanks to the truth behind this rule that formed in my consciousness after decades of fishing: How you fish a fly is at least as important as which fly you fish.

Another reason you can condense all those fly patterns down to a few is that lots of fly patterns will imitate one thing. For example, there are many imitations of the Blue-Winged Olive mayfly dun. All those flies accomplish the imitation a little differently, but they are, on the whole, interchangeable. Consequently, you don't need a Blue-Winged Olive Compara-dun and Blue-Winged Olive parachute fly and Blue-Winged Olive Thorax Dun and No-Hackle and all the rest. You just need *one* of these patterns, one solid imitation.

### BLUE-WINGED OLIVE IMITATIONS

So don't let those groups of curiously varied fly patterns calling from the bins of your local fly shop or the pages and pages of flies beaming up at you from the glossy paper catalogs or glowing from the Internet fly-fishing sites intimidate you. When you get to the specific types of fishing in chapters 7 through 10, I'll give you a sound basic list of fly patterns for each type, along with solid alternatives for when you can't find the specific patterns that are my first choices. In other words, I'll make fly selection easy. For now, just read on so that you understand flies in general.

Eventually you'll want more flies than the ones I'll recommend and will know how to use them, but for now, a box of only five to twenty-some flies will get you out fishing and catching fish.

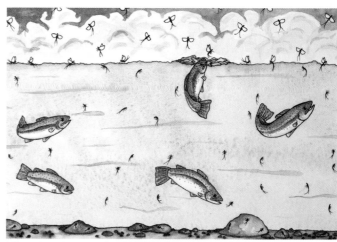

The abundance of a hatch often concentrates trout and sets them to serious feeding.

### Hatches and Imitative Flies

Usually, a solid familiarity with flies is enough to get you into fish. Other times, though... Fish really can get picky; a brown trout in a spring creek, for example—a naturally fussy trout in his fussiest environment—might ignore all but just the right sort of fly in just the right size. Fly-fishers call this single-mindedness "selectivity," meaning that a fish is selective, picky, about what it will and won't eat.

Selectivity is most common with trout, and usually occurs when one food-type is abundant. In lakes and rivers, many members of one particular insect species often make their metamorphosis from underwater pupae or nymphs to flying air-breathing adults as a mob, a flurry of action. Fly-fishers call this a "hatch." A hatch is important business on trout rivers and lakes—insects creep to the water's edge to struggle from their shucks, or just swim up in the open to squirm from them at the surface to stand atop still water or ride the currents as they unfold and dry their fresh new wings. Trout love hatches. When a hatch begins, they move to their feeding positions in rivers or go on the prowl in lakes. They get serious.

At first, the trout might key on the underwater form—so if you have a fly that looks like another one of those abundant identical nymphs or pupae on the move down there, and you fish it so that it imitates their movement, you'll probably catch trout.

As an open-water hatch builds (again, not all hatches are out in the open), the trout will probably move up to take partially hatched insects or adult insects at the water's surface. Each fish dents the face of the water whenever it gently noses down or *slams* down an insect, leaving a series of circular wavelets widening over the water, a "rise." Trout making rises with their feeding are "rising." To many trout fishers, fly fishing is really about rising trout.

Because of trout's tendency for selectivity (mainly during insect hatches) and because a broad variety of insects hatch in trout-water, most imitative flies are designed for trout fishing—there are tens, if not hundreds, of thousands of established trout-fly patterns.

A rise.

Imitative flies, like the dry fly on the top left, suggest a general or specific insect (as on the top right). Attractor flies, like the one in the bottom photograph, aren't supposed to imitate anything at all.

Trout aren't the only fish that will feed selectively. Smallmouth bass may jam their stomachs with immature crayfish and ignore plump dragonfly nymphs or baby smallmouth within easy reach. Largemouth bass may haunt the shallows to leap at mating dragonfly adults and ignore all else. Nearly all the varied fishes we seek with our flies are selective at times. Consequently, there are many imitative fly patterns for many different fishes.

Imitative flies fall into two general categories. The first is broad-purpose imitations—a dry fly flexible enough to imitate the adults of several pale mayflies, or perhaps an artificial nymph that suggests nymphs of both mayflies and small stoneflies, or perhaps a nymph-fly so rough and non-specific that it can pass as about any larva, nymph, or whatever.

The second category is *specific* imitations, not a fly that imitates just a big stonefly, for example, but only the blackish-and-orange Salmonfly stonefly, with the correct size and colors and shape to make the illusion complete.

Each category of flies has its place.

The broad-purpose imitations offer flexibility—keep some on hand and you always have *some* kind of reasonable imitation. The specific imitations offer an edge—if anglerwise, well-fed trout are nosing down identical Pale Morning Dun mayflies that are drifting in easy abundance on quiet currents, an imitation with all the right details may help you fool these nearly impossible fish.

But imitative flies are only half the story.

## Attractor flies

Attractor flies just make no sense. They are designed intentionally to *not* look like a real insect or a tiny fish or anything else a gamefish might actually eat. Some attractor flies appear vaguely insect-like or fish-like, but something's always out of whack—the colors are wrong or odd or the shape is unnatural in some way, or perhaps both. But unnatural as they are, attractor flies work. Sometimes they'll hook more fish than plausible imitative flies will hook—and occasionally, when imitative flies are useless, attractors will move fish after fish. I've seen it, many times.

Perhaps attractors work because they make fish curious. Perhaps they work because they offer the fish something new. We may never know why attractors work, but maybe it's enough just to know that they do.

On the whole, I suggest you try imitative flies first, something logical like a caddis-adult imitation for trout or a crayfish fly for smallmouth bass. But for most types of fly fishing you need to carry a few attractor flies and be ready to try them when imitative flies fail.

## Nymphs

"Nymphs" are sinking flies that imitate various larvae, pupae, real nymphs, and a few odds and ends, or are simply unnatural attractor designs that are normally fished just as

**Carey Special** (simple nymph)

**Kaufmann's BH Stone** (imitative nymph)

**Anatomical Golden Stone** (semi-realistic nymph)

**Gabriel's Trumpet** (attractor nymph)

**Pepperoni Yuk Bug** (attractor nymph)

imitative nymphs are fished. Both imitative and attractor nymphs range from tiny to big. To help nymph patterns sink, many have heavy wire inside their bodies; others have a head consisting of a metal or glass bead to pull them down. Some really heavy flies include both wire and bead.

But not all nymphs are weighted, or even meant to sink very deeply; some are fished barely under the water's surface in both rivers and lakes. In lake fishing, sinking lines typically do the work of drawing nymphs down, so lake-nymph patterns may carry little if any added weight. There are yet other situations in which a lightweight nymph is best, but in rivers, weighted nymphs are the norm.

## Emergers

Only a couple of decades ago, "emergers," flies that imitate insects in the process of shedding their shucks, were so few as to be something of a novelty. But insects half-bound by their vestigial skins are easy pickings for trout, and fly-fishers finally came to recognize it—today these flies are everywhere, and during hatches of mayflies, caddis, and midges it is now as common to fish emergers as dry flies.

Nearly all emerger-flies are imitative.

Morris Emerger
(mayfly emerger)

X Caddis
(caddisfly emerger)

Griffith's Gnat
(midge emerger)

Thunder Dome
(attractor emerger)

## Dry flies

"Dry flies" float, and traditionally stood high atop the water on the tips of the pointed fibers of feathers called hackles. While many still do, there are many dry flies now that rest most of their bulk down on the water's surface.

Most dry flies imitate mayflies, caddisflies, grasshoppers, and other insects. There are lots of attractor dry-fly patterns though, ranging from a little odd to plain crazy. Yet even the most bizarre attractor dries can be deadly under the right circumstances.

Both imitative and attractor dry flies are typically made with such buoyant materials as deer hair; synthetic furs; stiff, water-resistant feathers called "hackles"; and foam-sheeting loaded with tiny air-pockets. It's standard practice nowadays to rub a tiny amount of paste or liquid called "floatant" onto a dry fly (and even on the tippet) to maximize buoyancy. Floatant is commonly used on emergers too.

Goddard Caddis
(imitative dry fly)

Dave's Hopper
(big imitative dry fly)

Super Predator
(attractor dry fly)

## Streamers and bucktails

When I was a kid, flies that imitated little fishes fit neatly into two categories: "streamers," which had feather wings, and "bucktails," which had wings of long hairs from the tail of a deer. Now, many fish-imitations incorporate both hair and feathers and any number of synthetic fibers, and more. The old categories no longer work, so almost any fly that imitates a little fish is now called a streamer.

Fish eat fish, including their own offspring, and you can imagine how much protein a three-inch largemouth bass or rainbow trout provides—it'll take a heap of caddis pupae and scuds to match this much meat. Consequently, many of the sharpest fly-fishers carry streamers and use them, especially when there's no hatch or when they just want a shot at big fish. They may be trading steady hook-ups on thirteen-inchers with a nymph or dry fly for one heavy brown trout, but plenty of fly-fishers are fine with that bargain.

Black Ghost
(attractor streamer)

Little Rainbow Trout
(traditional bucktail)

Morris Minnow
(imitative streamer)

## Bass bugs

For largemouth bass and smallmouth bass, flies with buoyant deer hair flared and packed around their hooks and trimmed to various shapes—called "bass bugs" or "hair bugs"—are popular and effective. The standard bass bug comes in many forms: with a hair tail, with a feather tail,

| | |
|---|---|
| **Hair Bug** | **Dave's Swimming Frog** (diving hair bug) |
| **Near Nuff Crayfish** | **Clouser Minnow** (streamer) |
| **Popper** | **Foamtail Super Worm** (streamer) |

## BLUEGILL FLIES

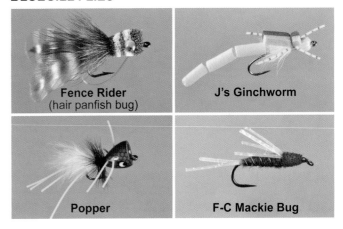

| | |
|---|---|
| **Fence Rider** (hair panfish bug) | **J's Ginchworm** |
| **Popper** | **F-C Mackie Bug** |

with rubber-strand legs or without them, with or without plastic eyes... Yet all the variations fall normally under the name bass bug. Most bass bugs imitate nothing, but some are shaped and colored to imitate frogs or mice; such specific imitations may have their own names...or not.

"Poppers" are basically bass bugs made of foam or cork or the like. They look something like lures, but they've long been categorized as bass flies. I prefer hair bugs, especially for largemouth bass, in part because hair is chewy and therefore more convincing than a hard cork or even foam popper—a bass is more likely to hang onto a hair bug for a while, giving me a better shot at setting the hook. Still, hard poppers catch a lot of bass, so use poppers all you like. I confess: I'm biased. I love lashing down and packing together dull and vivid colors of hair on a big hook, creating a pale belly and perhaps a dark back striped with yellow, and sculpting it all down to make something intriguing and lifelike. I'm more open to poppers on smallmouth rivers where currents can drench and sink a hair bug.

There are other fly types for bass, mostly streamers and such. But you already know about streamers. The other flies for largemouth and smallmouth bass imitate things they eat: crayfish, dragonfly adults, kind of crazy stuff sometimes.

Many flies for largemouth bass have a "snag guard," a strand of heavy monofilament arching under the hook point to protect it from catching on the lily pads and logs and other obstructions we throw bass flies into. You creep the fly over a branch but slam the hook past the guard when a bass takes. It actually works.

Flies for bluegills and other panfishes tend to look like miniature bass flies: hair bugs, poppers, streamers, but nymphs, some of them standard trout nymphs, too.

## Other flies

There are all sorts of flies for bonefish, tarpon, and other saltwater fishes, for Pacific salmon and steelhead, for carp (honest!), for muskellunge, for African tigerfish, and the list goes on. Once you've logged some real experience with trout or smallmouth bass or largemouth bass or bluegills—the fishes I'll soon teach you to catch—you may want to explore some of these less-common fly-fishers' species.

Besides flies for unusual fish, there are flies that are themselves pretty unusual and don't fit well into categories. Take the Glo-Bug, which sort of imitates an overly bright and usually oversize fish egg—is that a *nymph?* And the Flesh Fly Alaskans throw to Dolly Varden char eating shreds of the carcasses of spawned-out salmon. If the Flesh Fly's a streamer, it's a freakish one. There aren't many of these oddball patterns, but expect to run across one now and then.

| | |
|---|---|
| **Glo-Bug** (fish egg imitation) | **Flesh Fly** (salmon flesh imitation) |
| **Crazy Charlie** (bonefish fly) | **Undertaker** (steelhead & Atlantic salmon fly) |

# CHAPTER 3

# Knots and Rigging Up

Assembling your tackle to go fly fishing involves a lot of knot-tying, so we'll explore knots first. Funny thing about knots: they may confound you at first, but once you've got them you won't be able to remember what all the fuss was about. So, take them slowly. They'll come. Eventually you'll pretty much forget about them as you tie and select among them almost reflexively.

Because you'll typically change or replace flies at least a few times each day you go fishing, you'll need to be particularly adept at the fly-to-tippet knots (you'll find three such knots here).

The rest of setting up your tackle—connecting reel to rod, donning waders and wading boots, and the rest—are fairly straightforward. But figuring them out by the seat of your pants can be frustrating. The instructions in this chapter will make these tasks easy.

## KNOTS

You may eventually want to learn another knot or two, but the ones I'll teach you here are all you'll need for a long time, and most or all of them will always be part of your fishing.

Practice tying each knot one simple step at a time. Hold the ends of tippet and leader any way that works—between thumb and finger, two pinched fingers, whatever...

It's common practice to wet a knot in leader or tippet before tightening it (just dip it in the lake or river), to avoid abrasion that weakens the knot.

*Tighten* all knots by pulling *all* their ends, and give each of the parts a firm push from thumbnail or thumb and finger. Make sure a knot is tightly gathered up all around before fishing it.

*Trim* the stub-ends of a knot pretty close. I leave a very short cut end, only about 1/16-inch long, on all my knots. If you trim the ends off completely, the knot may fail if it adjusts itself even a little.

## Left- or right-hand reeling

Before you put the backing and line and leader on your reel (or have it done at a fly shop or by an online store), you need to decide which hand will do the reeling. Most fly reels can be switched so the drag resists in one direction or the other—"left-hand reeling," so that the reel-handle is on the left side of the reel as the caster holds the rod in the right hand, or "right-hand reeling," so that the reel-handle is on the reel's right side. So, which do you want?

Here's my advice, and the most common approach: if you are right-handed, set up your reel so the handle lies on your left, for left-hand reeling. If you are left-handed, set up your reel for right-hand reeling. This means you'll hold the rod in your dominant hand and work the reel with the other.

Some fly-fishers like to both handle the rod and work the reel with the same hand. This means they have to switch hands whenever they change from casting to reeling—which is often. Fine for them, and you may someday decide to join them. But for now, follow my advice.

**TIGHTENING AND TRIMMING KNOTS**

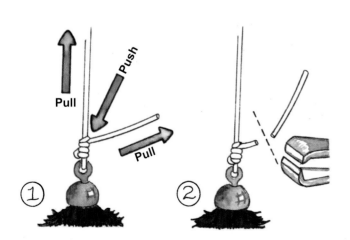

**BACKING-TO-REEL KNOT**

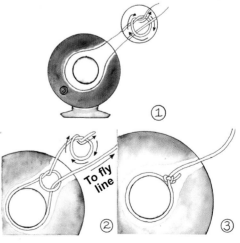

So simple: just two overhand knots. But tie it well because if this knot fails you could lose leader, fly, and an expensive fly line.

## NAIL KNOT

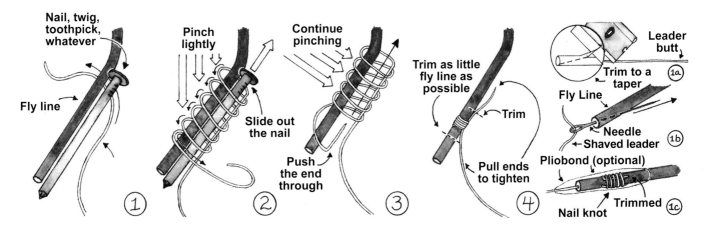

The nail knot connects backing to line, and tapered leader to line. This one takes real practice. First, cut off the leader's looped-end.

If your line comes with a looped end, just interconnect it with the looped end that comes on the butt of a leader—no nail knot.

## BLOOD KNOT

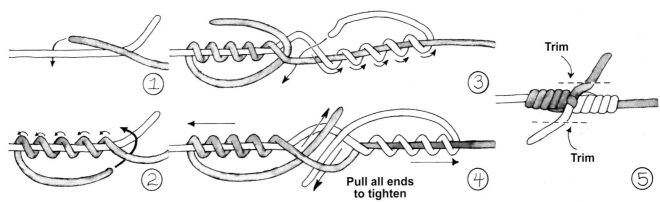

The butt of a tapered leader is normally attached to the tip of a fly line using the nail knot you just learned. But many fly-fishers just cut off the last leader they tied onto the fly-line (when its tip-end is worn out) to leave about a foot of the heavy butt section; they then tie each new leader to this short section using the blood knot above. Why?—a blood knot ties faster than a nail knot.

## SURGEON'S KNOT

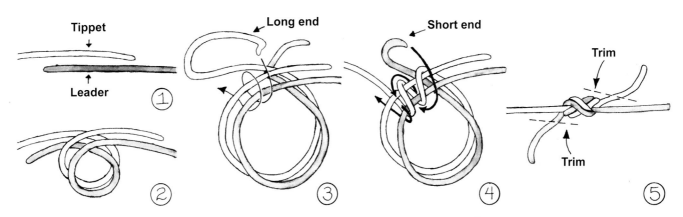

For attaching tippet to the fine point of a tapered leader, this knot is strong, quick, and the standard choice. Consider practicing it with two foot-long sections of heavy tippet (2X is good) before tying it with fine tippet and the fine point of a tapered leader.

## IMPROVED CLINCH (AND SKIP'S CLINCH)

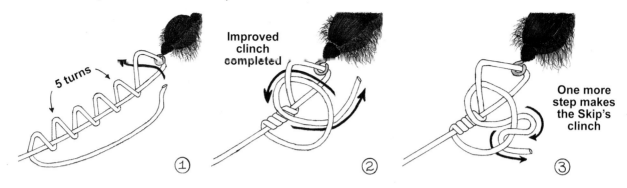

Here is your fundamental fly-to-tippet knot: the improved clinch. I and many fly-fishers have found the original clinch to be unreliable. Actually, I don't entirely trust the improved clinch—it's come back as a short, offending coil of tippet after losing me a good fish, and a fly, too many times. I've never had that problem with my Skip's clinch, formed simply by adding one more turn of tippet.

## MONO LOOP KNOT

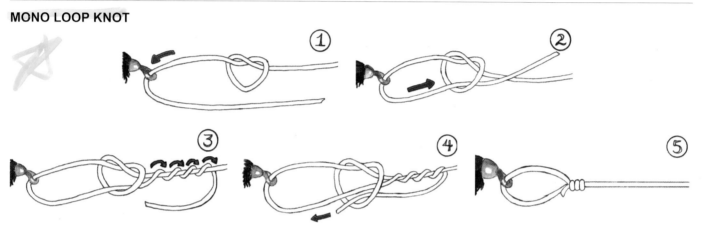

Because it allows a fly to shimmy and swivel, the mono loop knot has become very popular for nymph and streamer fishing of about any kind. Some even prefer it with a dry fly.

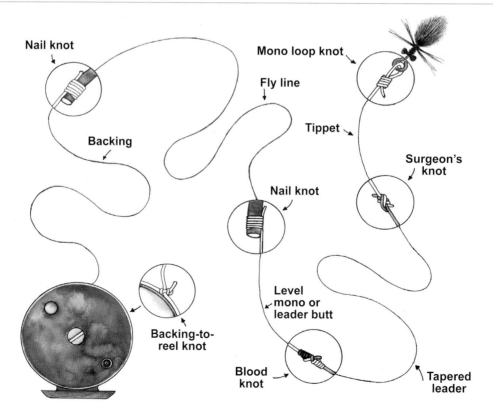

# RIGGING UP

Once you've got the backing and line and tapered leader and tippet all connected and set up on your reel (incidentally, unravel a new leader slowly, with care, or face a tangle), but before you can fix a strike indicator on your leader or tie on a fly, you'll need to assemble the sections of your rod and mount your reel on the rod's reel seat.

## Assembling the rod

To assemble your rod, you need to join the two sections of each ferrule. Your rod probably has either one ferrule, making it a two-piece rod, or three ferrules, making it a four-piece rod. Various ferrule designs have come and gone over the years, but today most have a smaller end on a lower section of a rod and a wider end on an upper section—the wider end slips over the smaller end. If your rod has some other kind of ferrule design, no problem; you'll easily figure it out.

If your rod has only one ferrule, hold the butt-section of the rod close to the male end of the ferrule and hold the tip-section of the rod close above the female end.

Push the two ferrule-parts *straight* at one another, so the rod-sections form a straight line the whole time. Push with *firm* pressure—too little pressure and the ferrule may later open while you're casting, causing the ferrule to break; but too much pressure and you may later have a tough time taking down the rod. Firm pressure is just right. Remember to always keep your hands near the ends of the ferrule as you push the ends together, because if your hands are too far apart, the rod may buckle and break as you push. But—*never* push on a guide, or you'll surely bend or break it.

If you have a four-piece rod, start by joining the tip-section with the upper-middle section. Join the center two sections; then the upper butt-section with the lower butt-section.

You want the guides aligned, so keep an eye on the guides as you join the ferrules. Many rods come with dots, or marks, near the ferrules—align the dots and you align the guides. Once the sections are all joined, you can hold the rod with the guides down, sight down the length of the rod, and see if any guides are angled off to one side or the other.

If the sections are misaligned, just pull the ferrule-ends apart and join them again in proper alignment. A slight misalignment is no problem, but a quarter-turn off *is* a problem.

The whole time you are assembling the rod, make sure you keep from setting it, even for a moment, in dust, dirt, or mud—anything that might cause abrasion on the guides or reel-seat parts. And you never want dust or dirt in the female or on the male ferrules. Also, be careful not to bang the rod against anything as you assemble it; those long rod ends need watching—they seem to love smacking a tree, wall, or fishing companion.

## Mounting the reel

The reel seat on the base of your rod will have a fixed ring or cap for one end of the reel's foot; it can be on either end of the reel seat. The other end of the reel's foot will be locked in a moveable metal ring that will tighten against the foot.

There are two ways that moveable ring normally tightens: (1.) the ring itself is threaded and you just screw it onto the foot, or (2.) the moveable ring is loose, with no threading, and a threaded ring behind it tightens to press it over the foot. Number 2 is the most common style.

To mount the reel on the reel seat, twist whatever ring is threaded so that it moves *away* from the *fixed* ring on the opposite end of the seat, to provide room for the reel-foot.

Now hold the reel so its foot is down against the reel seat, push the reel forward or back until the foot slips firmly into the fixed ring or cap. Next you have one of two options, depending on your style of reel-seat: (1.) screw the single threaded ring toward the reel's foot and tightly onto it, or (2.) push the loose ring firmly over the reel-foot, and then screw the threaded metal ring up against the loose ring until the reel is firmly mounted on your rod.

**JOINING THE FERRULES**

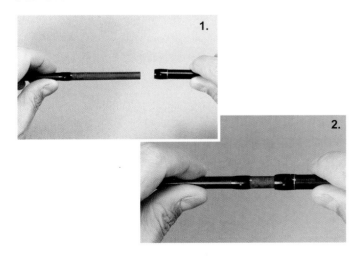

**MOUNTING THE REEL**

## Lining the rod

With the reel mounted in the reel seat, it's time to run the line and tapered leader and tippet up through the rod's guides. Start by finding the space in the design of the reel (there's always one thero, usually obvious) for the line to come straight out of the reel to the rod's lowest guide—the line shouldn't bend over or under any bar or frame-part of the reel.

Line coming properly off a reel

If your leader and tippet have been wound up onto the reel, rotate the reel's spool until you find the free end of the tippet—but don't pull on it. If you try to pull the line off the reel by the tippet, that fine tippet and the fine tip of the leader will likely bury themselves into the coils of line and make a tangled mess. So instead, pull *lightly* on the tippet as you *turn* the spool to slowly feed the tippet out. Continue doing this until all the tippet and tapered leader are entirely out of the reel.

Now you can do a little direct pulling on the fly line (and make sure the resistance, the "drag," of the reel isn't very firm. You can learn about setting the drag on page 38). Pull line steadily out of the reel, but don't rip it quickly or the spool may overrun and tangle the line. Just draw off line in slow to modest pulls until about 15 feet of line are out.

Set the mounted reel down on a table or *carefully* on the ground if, and only if, the ground is clean and you can be certain you won't get sand or dust into the reel's frame. The ground must also be soft, so that you won't scrape the reel. Grass or moss or wood are normally acceptable surfaces for your reel to rest on; rocks, concrete, dust, sand, and such are definitely not.

Double the fly line about a foot back from where it is attached to the tapered leader. Feed the doubled line up

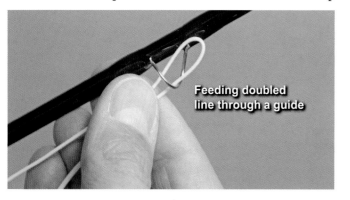

Feeding doubled line through a guide

through the lowest guide (the one nearest the reel) by pushing the loop up into the guide with one hand and grasping the loop on the other side of the guide and pulling it up through with the other.

Continue pushing the looped end of the line through each of the guides, from the lowest on up in sequence, and finally out of the tip guide. Pull all the loose line through the guides and out.

Now check your work. If you missed a guide or the line is wrapped around the rod, pull the line back out and start over again. This isn't complex; all will normally go well. Still, when you hear an experienced fly fisher grumble while rigging up, it's often because a guide was carelessly missed.

## Putting on waders

If you are about to fish a river, or fish a lake from a float tube, you need to put on your waders. Wear underwear, fairly loose pants (or sweat pants or insulated pants, depending on the weather and water temperature), and whatever's appropriate on your top half. Typically, you want to wear heavy socks, such as wading or hiking socks, in waders. The thick fabric insulates your feet against cold water and, in general, pads them through the knocking about of a day's wading.

Pull the tops of your socks up over the cuffs of your pants.

Step into the waders, pull them on, adjust their suspenders.

With loose-fitting waders (most waders) it's wise to wear a wading belt, as it helps keep your waders from swelling out with water if you fall in...a safety factor. So put one on and adjust it to where it will gather in the material and stay comfortably in place around your waist.

If your waders are the bootfoot type, you're done. But if yours are the typical stockingfoot type waders, you now need to put on wading boots. You can possibly lengthen the life span of your waders if you wear a second pair of socks outside the waders but inside the boots. Most fly-fishers don't wear this second pair though. Either way, just put on your wading boots as you would any boots.

## Float tubes and boats

To set up a float tube, V-boat, or kick boat, inflate all the chambers according to the craft's instructions. You can do this *carefully* with a service station's air hose (it's easy to overinflate and damage the seams with all that air pressure)—but only if your craft's instructions recommend it. Or you can use a portable pump.

Normally, you put the fins on over the bare feet of your stockingfoot waders. But there are fins that will fit over either bare waders or wading boots (and bootfoot wader-boots). Fins on stockingfoot-wadered feet are the least bulky and most efficient for movement; fins on boots increase protection for your waders' soft feet.

With a boat (or rowing kick boat), just set up the oars, make sure you have one life jacket per passenger, and row away. (Bring a life jacket for an inflatable craft too, if required by law or you just want the added safety.)

# CHAPTER 4

# Fly Casting

It would be difficult to *over*estimate the importance of casting to the fly fisher. I mean, if you can't get the fly out to the fish, the fish can't eat the fly, simple as that—and casting is the vehicle that carries the fly out there to the fish. Nearly always, the success of the whole fly-fishing process hinges on the cast.

Fortunately, fly casting really isn't all that difficult. I teach it one-on-one sometimes at sportsmen's and fly-fishing shows where I can normally get someone who's never held a fly rod to put out a presentable 35-foot cast after only 10 minutes of instruction. And a 35-foot cast is long enough to catch fish. In some situations it's longer than you need. Ten minutes, big deal.

The thing is, though, you want to be able to make a 35-foot cast fairly comfortably, without tangling everything up and without having to think much about what you're doing—*before* you actually go fishing. If you're trying to learn to cast and learn to fish at the same time, well, you probably won't do either one very well. It's like learning to drive in France while learning French. A sign comes up (let's say a stop sign) and you're struggling to translate it while trying to remember which pedal is the brake. Bad for you. Worse for French pedestrians using crosswalks.

My advice: put in at least four 10- to 20-minute practice sessions on casting, each session on a different day, before you go out and try to catch a fish. Six to eight sessions would be better...

But, honestly, don't let fly casting scare you. Follow the instructions I'll give you, take your time, reread them once or twice, and you'll probably do fine. If there are problems, keep *patiently* practicing and checking my instructions until things are working. Besides, fly casting becomes fun once you get the hang of it, almost meditative. The loop rolling gracefully down the line, the line dropping softly onto the water...

## HOW FLY CASTING WORKS

Sometimes it helps to understand how something works before you actually try it; I think this is one of those times.

Most other kinds of casting (spin casting, for example) depend on the weight of a relatively heavy lure to pull out a fine feather-light line, like throwing a baseball with a string attached. But *fly* casting depends on the weight of the thick *line* to carry out a feather-light (or at least fairly lightweight) fly. This makes fly casting a very different operation from other types of casting.

Another way to envision fly casting is to imagine the tapered fly line as a bullwhip. You snap the whip and a tight curve sails swiftly down its length to its fine tip. Same with a fly line.

What makes fly casting efficient is the line moving all in *one direction*. Poor casting habits will result in the line going in many directions—very inefficient. All the force of a champion arm-wrestler won't send a line out very far if the cast is bad. But the light, relaxed casting stroke of a child can push out 40 feet of line...so long as the kid's made a good stroke.

Fly casting is not—repeat: is *not*—about strength or speed. Although casting does require a little of both.

Successful fly casting is simply about good technique. And good technique in fly casting is really just about doing a few simple things right.

## THE BASIC FLY CAST

First is the standard, fundamental fly cast on which all the fancy ones are based—the one you'll probably rely on for most of your fishing for as long as you fly-fish.

Just follow the steps, and you'll learn the cast. And remember that a fly rod is a peculiar tool designed by man—it's unnatural, and making it perform properly requires your body to make unnatural movements. So pay attention, relax, take your time.

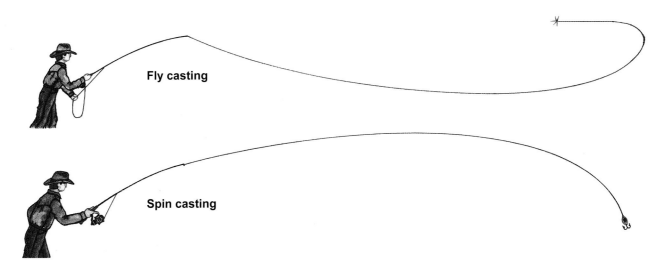

**Fly casting**

**Spin casting**

Rig your rod with the full-floating line and a tapered leader, pull out the line as described in caption #1 below, but instead of knotting on tippet, tie a one-inch length of yarn or ribbon on the end of the leader using a plain old square knot—no hooks yet! But wear glasses to protect your eyes from the snapping leader.

If your leader and line come off the reel in coils, hold the front three feet of the leader between your hands and stretch it firmly, until it is fairly straight; then stretch every three feet of leader and line you pulled out of the rod.

**1. Preparation:** Pick a still day, no breeze. A lawn is the best place to practice casting at first. Holding the rod's grip, strip line off the reel. Set the rod down flat on the lawn, and pull the line straight out in front of the rod—you want *15 feet of line* out of the rod's tip. (After you get the hang of casting, you can just cast out this line, but for now, pull it out.)

Pick up the rod (with your right hand if you are right-handed, with your left hand if you're left-handed). Keep the rod's tip down, close to the ground.

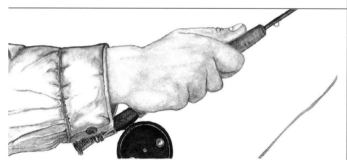

**2. Grip:** Hold the rod's grip, its handle, with your fingers curled around it and your thumb on top. The reel should be down, under the rod.

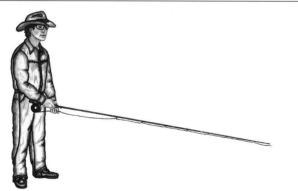

**3. Stance:** Stand comfortably erect. Step back slightly with the foot on the same side as your casting hand (the right foot for right-handers and vice versa). Now you should be standing so that you face the outstretched line but are turned slightly towards the rod. Keep the rod's tip down, so you don't pull in the line.

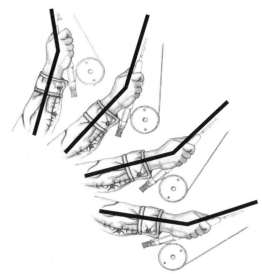

**4. Wrist:** Throughout the casting soon to come, you'll want to keep the wrist of your casting arm locked and unbending—*do not allow your wrist to bend even for a moment.* However, don't strain at the wrist—there is no need to tighten up. Just use the muscles lightly as required. Lock the wrist in a natural, straight position.

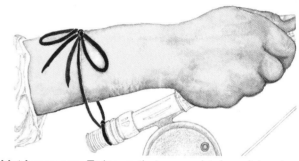

**Wrist Insurance:** To insure that your wrist doesn't bend as you cast (and to signal you when it does bend), tie about two-and-a-half feet of heavy string or cord in an overhand knot around the butt of your rod's reel seat. Hold the rod, and lightly pull the ends of the string up and tie them in a bow over your wrist (it's easier to have a friend tie the bow).

**5. The Clock:** Using the face of a clock to describe the casting arc of a fly rod is an old established approach—and an excellent one. We'll use it here.

The imaginary clock will be on your left side. Standing and holding the rod by its grip, as previously described, you want the rod's tip down just off the ground, the line straight out in front of you. (Left-handers: adjust the instructions to fit you.)

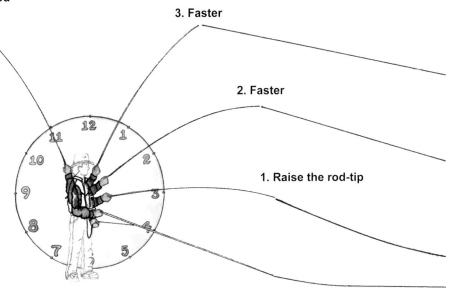

**4. *Stop* the rod**

**3. Faster**

**2. Faster**

**1. Raise the rod-tip**

**6.** Hold the line securely in your non-casting hand—*do not* let any line slip from that hand throughout the cast, or the cast will simply die. Use only the line you previously stripped off the reel; don't pull off more. Let your rod-arm relax naturally at your side, but with your elbow bent and your forearm and the rod forward.

Swing the rod's tip up and back in an arc (called the "back cast"), starting at modest speed and accelerating *steadily* to quick. When the rod reaches 11:00 o'clock (up to 10:00 o'clock), stop the rod there, suddenly and firmly—simply *stop* the rod.

Move both hands *together* on *every* stroke; keep them a constant distance apart.

**Wait...**

**7.** As soon as you stop the rod (at 11:00 to 10:00), the line will continue back and a loop will travel down the line.

Now, *wait*. It will take about one full second for the loop to roll most of the way out. (So, with 30 feet of line out you'd wait about two seconds, right?)

**When the loop starts into the leader,
begin your forward stroke**

**8.** Look back and watch the line. When the loop *starts* to roll off the end of the line and down *the tapered leader*, begin swinging the rod forward, slowly at first, but faster and faster (just as you did when you swung the rod *back*). Remember not to let the line *quite* fully straighten before starting the forward stroke (also called the "forward cast"). By the time the line and leader fully straighten, the line will start dropping. *Never* bend your wrist.

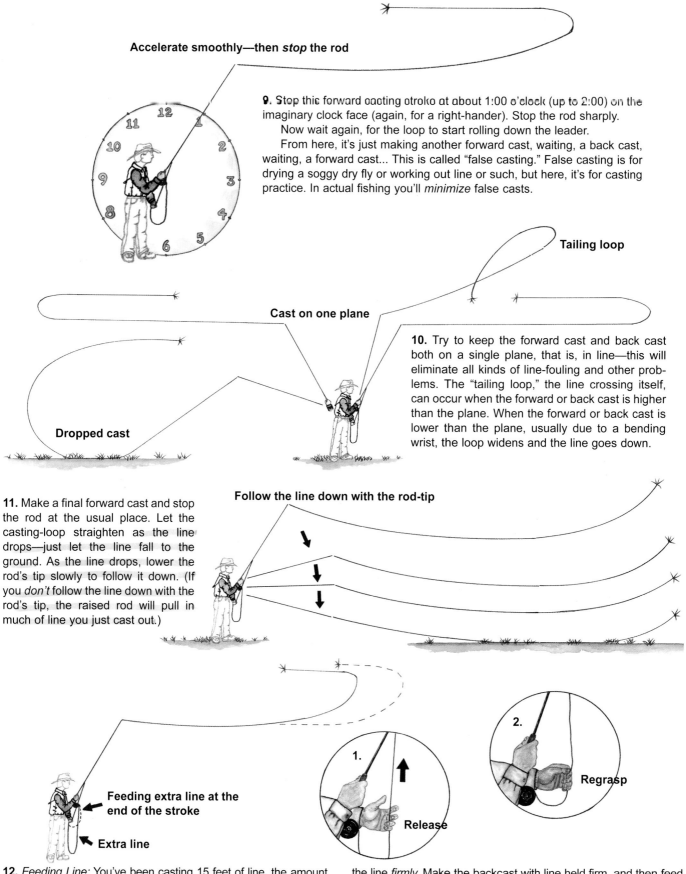

**Accelerate smoothly—then *stop* the rod**

**9.** Stop this forward casting stroke at about 1:00 o'clock (up to 2:00) on the imaginary clock face (again, for a right-hander). Stop the rod sharply.

Now wait again, for the loop to start rolling down the leader.

From here, it's just making another forward cast, waiting, a back cast, waiting, a forward cast... This is called "false casting." False casting is for drying a soggy dry fly or working out line or such, but here, it's for casting practice. In actual fishing you'll *minimize* false casts.

**Tailing loop**

**Cast on one plane**

**Dropped cast**

**10.** Try to keep the forward cast and back cast both on a single plane, that is, in line—this will eliminate all kinds of line-fouling and other problems. The "tailing loop," the line crossing itself, can occur when the forward or back cast is higher than the plane. When the forward or back cast is lower than the plane, usually due to a bending wrist, the loop widens and the line goes down.

**11.** Make a final forward cast and stop the rod at the usual place. Let the casting-loop straighten as the line drops—just let the line fall to the ground. As the line drops, lower the rod's tip slowly to follow it down. (If you *don't* follow the line down with the rod's tip, the raised rod will pull in much of line you just cast out.)

**Follow the line down with the rod-tip**

**Feeding extra line at the end of the stroke**

**Extra line**

**1.** **Release**

**2.** **Regrasp**

**12.** *Feeding Line:* You've been casting 15 feet of line, the amount you pulled off the reel, but you can lengthen your casts by "feeding" out line. To feed line, pull some line off the reel—three feet for now—and let it hang below your hand. At the end of the forward casting stroke let the line slip through your hand *briefly*—immediately *after* you stop the rod (never *before* you stop the rod). Release only about a foot and a half of line—and then quickly grasp

the line *firmly*. Make the backcast with line held firm, and then feed the other foot and a half out on the next forward stroke.

Pull in the three feet of line you fed out before practicing feeding line again.

Feeding line is about working a little of it out on every forward stroke. "Shooting line," coming next, is different—it's about firing out *all* the extra line on *one* stroke.

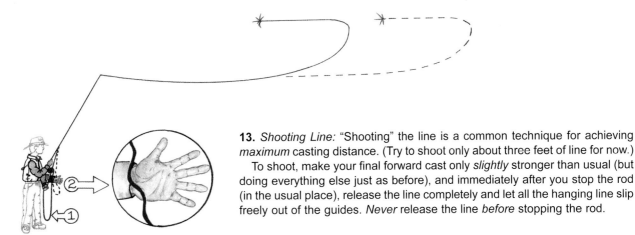

**13.** *Shooting Line:* "Shooting" the line is a common technique for achieving *maximum* casting distance. (Try to shoot only about three feet of line for now.)

To shoot, make your final forward cast only *slightly* stronger than usual (but doing everything else just as before), and immediately after you stop the rod (in the usual place), release the line completely and let all the hanging line slip freely out of the guides. *Never* release the line *before* stopping the rod.

## JUST THE BASICS

**Keep these seven points of casting in mind as you practice and your casting will almost certainly be smooth and efficient:**

**1.** Start each casting stroke slowly and accelerate gradually to fast, rather than casting in jerks. Accelerate smoothly.

**2.** Keep your hands the same distance apart throughout every casting stroke. If your hands come closer together on the forward stroke, line will slip out of the rod and the cast will die.

**3.** Stop the rod sharply on both back and forward casting strokes.

**4.** Never bend your wrist, not for a split second.

**5.** Follow the dropping line with the rod's tip to the water on the final casting stroke.

**6.** When either feeding or shooting line, always hold the line firmly, and then release it immediately after you stop the rod—never before.

**7.** Don't apply too much speed and force to your casts—many beginners do. But do apply enough speed, and turn your head to make sure you apply enough speed in both directions.

## Fine points

Sorry if this sounds repetitive, but again: strength and speed *are not* the key to successful fly casting. Still, it is possible to use too little force and speed—a bit of both is required. So if either your back cast or forward cast (could be either or both) collapse from insufficient energy, just add a little vigor where and when it's needed...a *little.*

Another worthy repetition—if you bend your wrist, all is lost. The loop widens and the line is thrown to the ground (or water). You really have to watch this because your body naturally *wants* your wrist to flex. (Yes, some advanced casting techniques involve a little wrist bending—but don't even *think* about that now.)

It's fine to angle the tip of the rod out away from you a little as you cast, but a little is plenty.

Classic error: trying to muscle the final forward cast before finally letting the line drop. It's human nature. When you dive into the cast like this you naturally lose all the technique you've learned and the cast fails. Remember that good casting comes not from brute force but from applying the principles you learned from this chapter.

A "tailing loop" is formed when the line crosses itself as the loop rolls down it—the result is usually the fly caught on the line. A rushed casting stroke, one the rod can't keep up with, can cause the problem. The cure is to make your casting strokes not hurried jabs but smooth accelerations building speed right up to the point at which you stop the rod. (And, again, keep your forward and back casts on a single plane.)

The line follows the rod's tip, so if you swing the rod too far back or too far forward the loop in the line will open wide and the line will head for the ground.

Try not to *twist* the rod you cast—this will make casting inefficient and inaccurate, and can also twist the rod-sections out of alignment. The solution is to watch your reel as you practice. If the reel swings up to one side, you're twisting.

Turning your head as you cast, to watch both your forward and back casts, is an excellent idea. You'll be amazed at what you'll see when you do: a bending wrist, an under or overpowered stroke, a jerking cast rather than a smooth increase of speed...

Lots of false casting is a great way to practice fly casting. But fishing is another matter—"You can't catch fish with the fly in the air," seasoned fly-fishers like to say, and they're right. One or two false casts is usually enough to deliver the fly. Just one back cast is even better. (Though, of course, you'll sometimes need a few false casts to dry a fly or feed out line.)

Extra snap is required on whichever end of the cast is thrown into a good wind. If the wind is coming at your casting-arm side, you can angle the rod across your chest, away from the wind. A bit awkward, but it keeps the line from being blown against you.

The longer the cast, the longer the casting strokes. But on short casts, the rod's tip shouldn't travel far. Also: the longer the cast, the longer the wait between strokes; and use *slightly* more speed and force for a long cast than for a short cast.

You'll often need to change the direction of your casts. To do this, just aim each forward stroke a little further towards the target direction. A few false casts should do it.

When you practice casting you can watch the rod, but in fishing, especially if accuracy is important, you look primarily not at the line but at the spot where you want the fly to go.

When you do eventually cast on water (which you can try any time, really) you'll find that the water will grip the line, requiring a little extra force to get it moving and up in the air. A wet line will also feel slightly heavier than a dry line.

Often, you'll wind up on the wrong side of the river. For a right-hander this means fishing upstream from the right bank. The solutions: 1. wade or cross a bridge to the other side and fish from there (if you can) 2. angle the rod across your chest (for a right-hander the rod would then angle off the left shoulder) or 3. learn to cast with the other hand (but don't even consider this until you've become a solid caster with your favored hand).

It's always a good idea to look behind you before you cast, to avoid snagging your fly in a tree or a friend or whatever.

On smaller streams, or in a tight spot within brush or tree limbs or such, you may do best not to cast at all but to "dap," simply reach out with the rod, only a few feet of leader and tippet beyond the tip, and *set* the fly on the water. Hold the line up close to the bottom stripper guide as you dap, or the line will drop, dragging the fly up to the rod's tip.

## SLACK-LINE CASTS

On trout rivers, most flies are fished "dead drift," that is, drifting as though free in the current, as though unattached to tippet. Flies are also occasionally fished dead drift in rivers for small-mouth bass and other fishes. The problem with achieving dead drift is that currents are always uneven, angling this way and that, shifting and rushing and slowing alongside one another—and all this pulls at the line and leader and tippet to draw the fly off its natural course. Fly-fishers call this unnatural fly movement "drag." Even a little drag can alert a cagey trout.

The way to avoid drag (or at least delay it) is to put waves and coils—"slack"—in the line, leader, and tippet. Then the fly can drift freely for as long as the current is busy drawing out the slack. True dead drift.

Because the tippet is level, untapered, it naturally tends to drop onto the water in loose curves. To add even more slack to a tippet, just cast a little higher off the water, so the tippet has plenty of time to curl as it drops. A long tippet also helps provide slack.

Putting slack into the fly line is about casting, making slack-line casts. However, this is too soon for you to be learning several additional casts. So I'll teach you one trustworthy, time-proven slack-line cast that is versatile and will serve you honorably: the S or lazy S cast.

(One effective alternative to slack-line casting, and the mending you'll soon learn, is to reach out and up with the rod and simply *hold* the line above a tricky piece of current. Most times it's not enough, but sometimes it's just right.)

### JUST THE BASICS

**Here are the main points behind making the S cast:**

1. Make a normal forward cast.
2. Immediately after you stop the stroke—but no sooner or later—start waggling the rod side to side.
3. Keep the waggles narrow and quick.
4. Follow the line down to the water with the rod's tip.

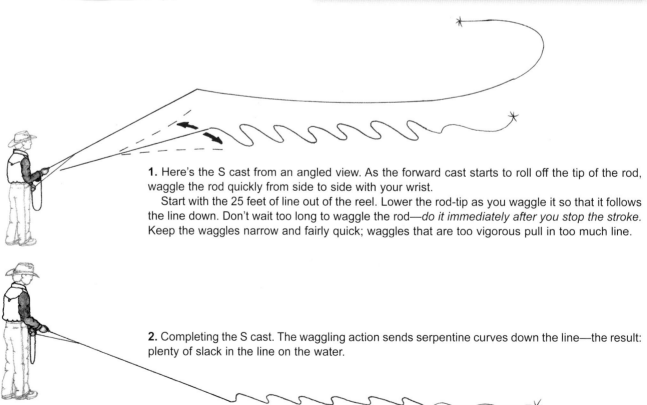

**1.** Here's the S cast from an angled view. As the forward cast starts to roll off the tip of the rod, waggle the rod quickly from side to side with your wrist.

Start with the 25 feet of line out of the reel. Lower the rod-tip as you waggle it so that it follows the line down. Don't wait too long to waggle the rod—*do it immediately after you stop the stroke.* Keep the waggles narrow and fairly quick; waggles that are too vigorous pull in too much line.

**2.** Completing the S cast. The waggling action sends serpentine curves down the line—the result: plenty of slack in the line on the water.

# MENDING

Those shifting river currents I mentioned in my introduction to the S cast may eventually take out almost any amount of slack you can put into the line and leader and tippet. If the slack you need is going away, you can "mend" the line—give it a flip to make it curve upstream or downstream. Sometimes a straight, standard fly cast followed by a mend is more effective than an S cast—it all depends on how the currents play. For example, if there's a quick thread of current between you and the slower water you want your fly to drift through drag-free, an immediate mend upstream will throw a curve in the line that will put off drag. If that thread of current in the center is *slower* than the water beyond it, mend downstream.

Mending is handy with dry flies and emerger flies, nymphs with strike indicators, and streamers.

Expect your dry fly or emerger fly to make a little hop when you mend. As long as the hop is short and brief, no problem. Mending, during casting practice or actual fishing, requires the grip of water, so don't waste your time trying to learn it on a dry lawn—wait until you're on a pond, river, or lake.

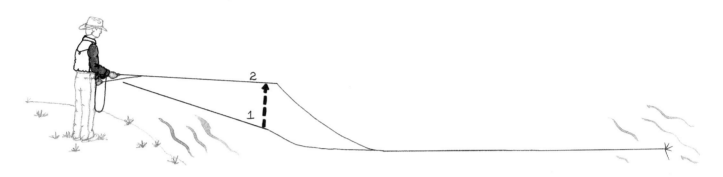

**1.** Mending: Start with the rod's tip down near the water and the rod aiming straight down the line. Raise the rod's tip slowly to draw some of the line up off the water.

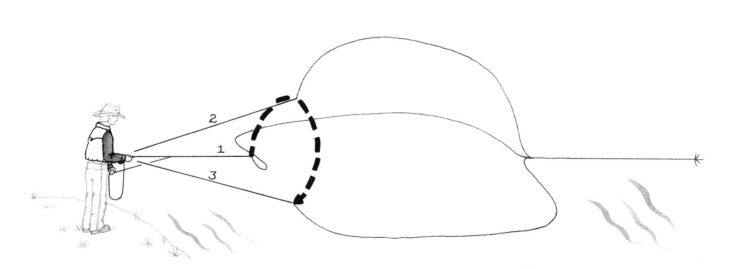

**2.** Flip the rod's tip sharply to your side—and then *stop* the rod abruptly, as you would at the end of a cast. The rod's tip should move up and back down, in a sort of half-circle. Accelerate the stroke much as you would with a standard cast.

The line should rise as it travels in a half-circle. The line should drop with a pronounced curve, a "belly," fly-fishers call it.

Worth repeating: you can only mend or practice mending on water—it won't work without water's resistance.

# CHAPTER 5

# Finding Fish

The specifics on where to find particular fishes in rivers and lakes will come soon in the four chapters that each cover a different way to begin fly fishing. In this chapter, you'll learn how to, as anglers like to say, "think like a fish." The debate about whether or not fish actually do think aside, the point is for you to understand why fish go where they go and do what they do—know this, and you know how to find the fish you want to catch. Think-like-a-fish is a notion that has served a great many fishermen extremely well for decades, at least. It creates a mind-set that can really pay off.

## SAFETY

Depth helps protect fish from predators.

So, now that you're thinking like a fish, what's your first priority? To survive, of course. Surviving will mainly amount to avoiding predators. So, look at a lake or river—if you were a fish in that water, where would you go to avoid predators? Where would you be safest?

Depth brings a certain degree of safety; it's hard for a bird or otter to reach you deep in a lake or a big pool in a river.

Little fish like cover in shallow water.

If you're a little fish, though, a baby trout or bass, deep water may be the most dangerous place of all—that's where the big trout and bass lie, and they'll chase you down and eat you without a flicker of hesitation. And in that open water there'll be no "cover," that is, anything you can use for protection or hiding. At the edges of a lake or river are fallen trees and rocks to hide among, and the big fish will be reluctant to expose themselves to otters and birds and such in shallow water. But now *you're* in range of those otters and birds. Still, it's better than lying in the open down with big hungry fish. Yes, the shallows, among the water plants and rocks and fallen timber, that's the safest place for you if you're a little fish.

These are the sorts of things you understand if you think like a fish, and when you do, it's suddenly plain why big fish tend to hold deeper but little fish tend to hang around the shallows.

Still thinking like a fish (specifically, a fish of some size, since that's the sort of fish you want to catch) you know at some instinctive level that in flowing water—rivers, streams, creeks—there is not only depth for protection, there's current. It's difficult for predators to see through current and difficult for them to attack through it as well. So lying in or alongside good currents can help keep you alive.

## FOOD

And there you are, an adult fish, as safe as you're going to get, down in the depths of a river or lake. But where's the food? safety isn't everything; you must eat to survive.

In a typical lake, most of the food lives in water from a few inches to fifteen or twenty feet deep, where light reaches down to grow water plants and the insects and crustaceans that inhabit them; these, in turn, attract the larger predacious insects, minnows, leeches, and other creatures that feed on them. You, a fish, will of course eat all of these. So you need to regularly visit that shallow to only modestly deep water. Trout and largemouth and smallmouth bass regularly enter the shallows of lakes. But leaving deep water for shallower water puts you in range of those pesky, carnivorous, life-threatening predators I mentioned.

It's much the same in rivers—tiny delectable fishes wait for you in the shallows but the shallows are dangerous; the depths are much safer.

Feeding at the surface is dangerous too—you're exposed to birds from above and anything coming up from below.

So you'll have to take chances in order to satisfy your stomach. One strategy: go to the shallower water or the surface when the light is low—on overcast days, at sunset and sunrise, and at night. And you know instinctively that even a little cloud-shade makes it much harder for ospreys and other large hunting birds to accurately soar down to stab you with their claws.

Low light provides protection from predators.

Another strategy: stay close to cover—a fallen log you can dart around to escape and that obscures you from predators' eyes, lily pads that make it difficult for a predator to spot you or track your movements... So as the risk rises in shallower water, you'll seek the protection of cover, low light, or both.

Cover, of all sorts, means survival to gamefish.

Cover, shade: even with these working for you, predators are cunning and always ready to strike—so watch out, and be always ready to flee for your life! If food is abundant in the open, it may be worthwhile to just look around, and then, if it feels okay, to slide cautiously out to quietly feed. But if you see any sign at all—a flicker of shadow, a splash, or a crunch or a thump you feel, "hear," with the sensitive receptors along your flanks—bolt for the protective depths or the nearest cover.

This is why fish in shallow water, especially in clear water under strong light, are normally so jumpy and easy to spook.

## OXYGEN, TEMPERATURE, AND COMFORT

Okay, you're still a fish, and you have to breathe oxygen, another matter of survival, really. So you find and stay within water holding a comfortable oxygen level. A river turned small and warm by summer's dry heat will be oxygen-poor in its deeper, slower sections. It you have a trout's heavy need for oxygen, you'll have to avoid these quiet areas. You'll find the most oxygen in the quick,

broken water. That thinner water may not be as safe from predators as the deep pools, but...you know...breathing isn't optional.

In a lake, this gets more complicated, especially if you're an oxygen-loving trout. The shallows will be well oxygenated in the cool of spring and fall, but low in oxygen during the hot days of summer. So in summer and early fall you'll be able to feed in the shallows only during the chilly mornings and evenings and at night, since cold water can hold more oxygen than warm water.

And then there's "stratification," the water dividing itself into different layers of temperature. You'll have to stay within the levels that provide you comfortable—or at least survivable—levels of oxygen.

If you're a small- or largemouth bass or one of the panfishes, you won't need as much oxygen as a trout, but you still have your limits, so the principles that determine when and where oxygen collects apply to you too.

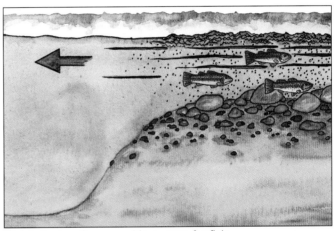
Quick, broken flows provide oxygen for fish.

On the whole, thinking like a fish boils down to the principles we just explored. They may not mean a lot to you right now, but one day you'll be looking at a lake or river, wondering where the fish might be, and suddenly you'll think, *Oh...of course...*

### JUST THE BASICS

**Here are the principles behind thinking like a fish, summed up:**

**Survival:** mainly about light and cover, food, and oxygen

**Light and cover:** bright light, high predator danger; low light, low predator danger. Cover always increases safety

**Food:** always important, but it's not always in safe places

**Oxygen:** moves around with temperature, stratifies in lakes. Oxygen is higher in quick, broken currents than in slow ones.

# CHAPTER 6

# Hooking, Playing, and Landing Fish and Such

I recently watched a beginning fly fisher select and tie on an appropriate fly and then cast it out in front of a trout, all with solid competency—and then lose that trout, and another, and another. A few more fish would have escaped had I not stepped in. The problem lay in her hook-setting and playing; both were just too timid. After a little instruction the young woman began hooking, landing, and releasing fish successfully. But I've seen this go the other way too—losing fish to overaggressive hook-setting and playing.

The elements of fly fishing must fall like a wave down a toppling line of dominoes if fish are to be hooked and landed—one gap in the process and the wave stops and the fish is off.

That's not to say that playing and landing a fish on a fly rod, or fly fishing in general (even if a few elitists want you to believe otherwise) is almost impossibly difficult. Normally, it isn't, not even close—I've seen newcomers land fish after fish on a fly. But they succeeded because they did certain things correctly, or at least adequately.

So we'll make sure you do those certain things correctly by examining the critical fly-fishing dominoes.

## RETRIEVING THE FLY

Dry flies and emerger-flies and nymphs in rivers are usually fished dead drift, with the angler working to *avoid* moving the fly. But what about streamers and the various sunken flies and all sorts of other flies that must dart or swim or hop or sputter? Most of those need to be "retrieved," that is, animated by drawing in fly line.

River currents or the drift of your float tube or boat on a breezy lake can fool you—you may be drawing in line but the fly may not be moving. The test: look at your line; if it's not moving, neither is the fly; you need to retrieve faster.

Here are the standard methods of retrieving flies.

### Strip Retrieve

Stripping line is the most natural retrieve—most fly-fishers just figure it out on their own. To strip in a fly, hold the line lightly between your curled first finger (or first and second fingers) and the underside or side of the rod's grip (or between the finger and thumb of your rod-hand). Reach forward with your other hand, grasp the line below your rod-hand, pull it down and back, release the line, reach up and regrasp it, and pull more line back through the rod's guides...

The advantages of the strip retrieve, or "stripping," are that it's easy and natural, and it can take in line slowly to quickly. The disadvantage is that fish may hit the fly at that vulnerable point when your hand is reaching for the line. Never release the line from your rod-hand as you strip it.

**STRIPPING LINE**

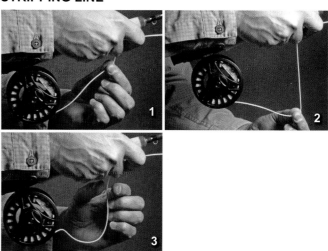

### Hand Twist

Here's a line-and-fly retrieve with no weak spots—the hand-twist retrieve provides a secure and constant hold on the line. It's a slow retrieve, which for many flies is just right. The difficulty of doing the hand twist with any real speed can be a gift to beginners, who tend to retrieve a fly too quickly—often, *way* too quickly.

Hold the line in your rod-hand, as with the strip retrieve. Grasp the hanging line between the thumb and first finger of your other hand, rotate your thumb and finger down and away from the rod with a twist of the wrist to pull in a few inches of line, catch the line with your little finger, and then with another twist of the wrist swing the little finger down to pull in some more line. Don't hold the line in your palm; let it drop after each pull.

**HAND-TWIST RETRIEVE**

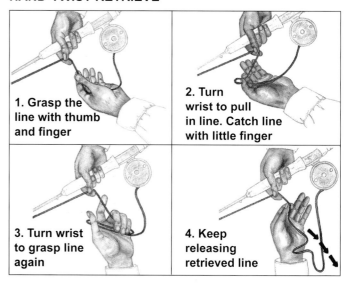

1. Grasp the line with thumb and finger

2. Turn wrist to pull in line. Catch line with little finger

3. Turn wrist to grasp line again

4. Keep releasing retrieved line

## SNAGS

Lakes, rivers, saltwater bays—wherever you're throwing your fly, it may hook all sorts of things that are not fish. When your fly catches on a high branch or down between boulders or deep on a lily pad or whatever, point your rod straight down the line, hold the line firmly, and then pull back on the line, pulling steadily harder until the fly comes free or the tippet breaks. Fact is, if you fish, you lose flies. Of course if you can safely pull down a tree limb or wade out or row out and free your fly, go ahead. (Sometimes tugging, *not* pulling hard, on the fly from different angles will free it.)

## SETTING THE HOOK

### How Hard

When a fish takes your fly, swing the rod up and back to drive the point of the hook home—fly-fishers call that "striking" (which is a little confusing at first because when a fish hits the fly they'll call that a strike too). That's the basic idea, but there's more to it.

How hard do you set the hook? That depends on some variables, so you'll get specific answers in chapters 7 through 10 on the four kinds of fishing we'll explore. In general, though, you *always* set the hook hard enough to fully sink the point of the hook into the fish's mouth. If you're fishing a tiny size-22 dry fly, a light tug will do it right. On the other hand, if you're fishing a big bass bug with a monofilament snag guard, you'll need to slam the hook's point past the stiff mono.

Then there's tippet strength to consider. If the tippet is light, say 6X, you can't apply much pressure or you'll break off your fly. But with stout 1X tippet (for that big bass bug I mentioned in the last paragraph) you can really put some power into the hook-set—but, except for big largemouth bass flies and the enormous flies for some man-size saltwater fishes, you'll never come even close to throwing all your strength and body weight into a hook-set.

Typically, the bigger the fish, the larger the fly and the harder the hook-set. Though the difference in the force you'll apply between a 10-inch trout and a 20-inch trout may be little or, if both fish take the same size-14 dry fly, none. I'm talking about *big* differences in fish size.

There are a few miscellaneous factors. Fishes with hard mouths, such as pike and barracuda (you'll read about them in chapter 12), naturally require a hard hook-set and stout tippets to match. Fishes with soft mouths, such as the freshwater crappie (also in chapter 12), require a light hook-set; otherwise the fly will tear free. With really small fish, such as trout in a creek or five-inch sunfish, a hard hook-set can send the poor fish flying over your shoulder. Sometimes your hook-set isn't about the fish at all, but about your rig—if you're nymph fishing a trout river with a strike indicator; big, heavy split shot on the leader; and a big weighted fly, you'll need to strike pretty hard and with a long enough stroke to get all that junk moving so the weighted fly on the end of it jumps into the trout's jaw.

### How Soon

How soon after the fish takes your fly do you set the hook? That varies. If you're fishing a nymph in a river, you set the hook just as soon as possible after the strike indicator tells you a fish has taken your fly. That's because the indicator speaks late, leaving barely enough time to get the job done. But if a trout is peacefully sipping tiny insects at the surface, you'll probably find that a half- to one-second pause before setting the hook allows him time to draw in the fly and close his jaws. Generally, set a sunken fly immediately, but pause with a floating fly. And always be willing to experiment.

You'll find the specifics on how quickly to set the hook in the four chapters on specific types of fishing.

Regardless of whether or not you pause to set the hook, the *action* of setting the hook should be swift, a quick tug.

The basic hook-set is just a sudden (usually light) raising of the rod's tip. You can do this by bending the wrist, bending at the elbow, or both. The important thing is that the rod's tip moves quickly—but not necessarily with much force—and travels far enough to give the fly a tug. If the hook-set doesn't pass its energy through the line, leader, and tippet to the fly, it won't drive the hook's point home.

Hard hook-sets may require yanking back on line and rod both, as with largemouth bass and snag-guard flies.

## JUST THE BASICS

**Here's a rundown on setting the hook:**

**How hard:** In general, with flies of size-16 and smaller and tippets of 6X and finer, set the hook lightly; with flies of size 14 to 8 and tippets of 5X to 3X, set the hook firmly; with hooks of size 6 and larger and tippets of 2X and heavier, set the hook from hard to very hard.

**Fish size:** Although hook-size and tippet-thickness come first, in general set the hook from lightly on small fish to hard on big fish.

**How soon:** Immediately on sunken flies, *usually* after a pause with floating flies.

# PLAYING A FISH

Remember this: the most important factor in playing fish (with one exception) is keeping *constant* pressure on the line, enough pressure to tire the fish and keep the fly pulled tight—but never enough pressure, even for a moment, to break the tippet.

And you want to avoid *over*playing a fish; that is, you want to land the fish as soon as reasonably possible—a fully exhausted fish may not survive. (Flies with hook-barbs absent or smashed down also help fish survive after being caught.)

## Setting the drag

The reel's drag largely determines how much pressure you put on the line and, therefore, the fish—*if* the fish is large. With a six-inch bluegill or a ten-inch trout you'll likely do all the fighting while just *holding* the line. But hook a crazy 20-inch rainbow trout in the open water of a lake and you'll be working off the reel in moments—if the drag is too tight that fish will break off your fly; if the drag is too loose the reel will over-run itself and tangle, which will lock up the reel and there goes that 20-incher with your fly.

**FLY REEL DRAGS**

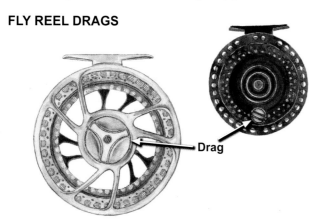

Different reels have different systems for adjusting their drags. Some reels have a little knob on their edge that twists, others have a large disk on the back of the frame that twists, and others have a lever that clicks from one position to the next. All that really matters is that you read the instructions that come with your reel, find the drag-setting knob or lever, and adjust it properly.

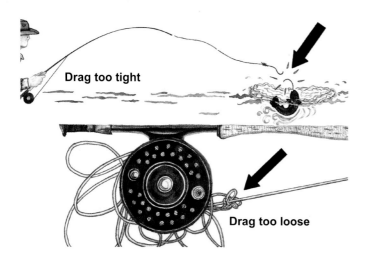

A properly set drag allows you to pull line off the reel at a resistance below the breaking strain of your tippet. Setting the drag to this level gets easier with experience, but it's pretty straightforward overall—tighten the drag, pull some line off the reel, and if the line comes off only with such a hard pull that your tippet would break if it were tippet you were pulling, the drag is too tight. You can always cut off some tippet, tie an overhand knot in it, and then pull the ends until the tippet breaks to get a sense of how tightly to set your drag so the tippet is safe.

Theoretically this means that with thick 0X tippet for big largemouth bass back in the weeds, your drag will be set tight. The problem with this is that pulling line off the reel as you fish will become a chore. So with heavier tippets, most fly-fishers set the drag only to firm, and then they palm the reel (see chapter 1, page 10) or quickly adjust the drag down tighter when they hook a fish.

Clearly, there's a big range for setting the drag, and it's mostly about tippet strength—at the light end, with 6X tippet or finer, you might set the drag so soft that its resistance is barely noticeable; at the heavy end, with 2X tippet or stouter, you might set the drag as hard as you can without having to strain to pull off line for casting.

## Fish on!

So, you're standing in a river, the drag on your reel is correctly adjusted, and you just set the hook in a trout. You're holding the rod in one hand and the line in your other hand, with a few feet of extra line trailing downstream on the current.

If that's a medium-size trout, say a 13-incher, you'll normally play him off the extra line hanging below your hands. The fish runs, you let the line pull out of your grasp with some resistance. When you can work the fish in, you hold the line lightly in your line-hand, and strip some line in through the finger (or fingers) and thumb (or rod grip) of your rod-hand. Remember, as you reach for the line each time, to take the line not *above* but *below* your rod-hand. So, you grasp the line each time, and strip it in.

Small fish are easy. With a five-inch bluegill or eight-inch trout, just resist the fish a little while until it tires. No line screeching off the reel, no pressing the tippet to its limit. Easy.

But let's say the trout is big and *really* runs. What do you do?

You need to get the trout onto the reel. So, you hold the line in your line-hand only firmly enough to keep good tension on the fish—but not enough tension to risk breaking the tippet. The fish keeps running, taking out more line. The line that was dangling below the rod is about gone; this means the fish will suddenly come up hard against the stationary reel.

You have to cushion the switch from held line to reel otherwise the tippet may break before the reel's spool can overcome inertia and start turning. Here's how:

1. With the hanging line all but gone (not too soon...), release the line from your line hand altogether (or guide it with a loop formed by your thumb and first finger).
2. As you release the line, lower the rod's tip to soften the transition from held line to spool.
3. Just let the fish keep running and pulling more line off the reel. You can palm the spool if you need to increase drag or, if the reel has no palming rim, you can pinch the line a little as it runs out.

That's it. Now just let the fish run until he tires and stops.

Good start, but you're not done yet. You need to work, "pump," the fish back in—lower the rod's tip as you reel in some line, raise the rod's tip, lower it as you reel in more line... When the trout ends its run, try pumping in a little line, to see if you can coax the fish your way; be careful though—the trout could suddenly run again at any time, and if he does, let go of the reel's handle immediately to let him take line. When the run stops, resume pumping in the trout. But the trout may run again—perhaps several more times—probably when you don't expect it.

Important: whenever the trout runs, let go of the *reel's handle completely*. If you even touch the reel's handle during a run, the tippet will probably break.

Trout, largemouth bass, and sometimes smallmouth bass (and, in fact, many fishes) will jump up to shake wildly in the air. It's a good tactic...for them. But if you lower your rod tip to slacken the line and leader as the fish leaps, the odds of the fish breaking your tippet go down. Slack line is particularly important with a large fish—that big tail can really take out a tippet.

But, other than during jumps, keep the pressure on the fish *constant*—one moment's slack and he may spit the fly.

Throughout the fight (except when you drop the rod tip for a jump), keep the rod up at about a 45° angle to the line so the flex of the rod helps you protect the tippet. Only when you're really wrestling a fish on a heavy tippet, as you might with a largemouth bass straining towards a log, will you drop the rod-tip and pull hard. It's a sort of desperation move you seldom use with most fish (though often with a few fishes).

Although I used a trout as an example, that's about how it goes with playing almost any large fish.

**Slackening the line on a jumping fish**

## JUST THE BASICS

### Here's a rundown on playing a fish:

- Adjust the reel's drag properly.
- Keep the pressure on, not so much pressure you risk breaking the tippet, but not far short of that either.
- Drop the rod-tip as loose line runs out and tight line hits the reel during a fish's run.
- When a fish wants to run, let it.
- When a fish is running, don't touch the reel's handle.
- After the fish has stopped running, try pumping it in—but be ready to let it run again at any moment.

Play a fish with your rod at a right angle to the line.

## LANDING A FISH

When your fish is tired and ready to come in, you need to know to how control him so you can remove the hook and return him unharmed (it's called catch-and-release—you'll learn about it on page 74).

To land a trout (or any other fish) with a net in either a river or lake, play the fish until he is tired enough to come to net (remember: tired but not exhausted). Raise the rod high and slide the trout in on its side, with its head angling up.

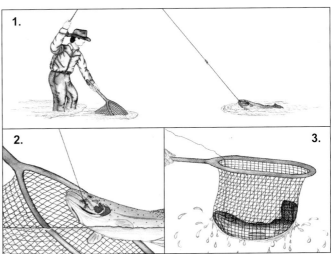

Have the net already extended towards the fish with the front of the rim well below the surface of the water. When the trout comes over the net, simply raise the net—fish landed.

If the trout won't slide in as I've described, it's not ready for the net. Never poke at a fish with the net, you'll just lose the fish.

Avoid pulling the line-to-leader connection inside the tip guide—it can catch there, and then if the fish runs... trouble.

If you have to hold a trout, *do not squeeze it*—that's an anguished death sentence for the fish. Imagine an elephant stepping on your stomach—it'd be awfully easy for that giant to unintentionally crush your innards... So hold your stiff fingers around the trout without *squeezing*, even for a moment.

Most fly-fishers don't net largemouth or smallmouth bass. Instead they grasp the fish quickly by its lower jaw, with their first finger curled sideways under the jaw and their thumb inside on top, and lift. When you lift a bass this way, it usually freezes, making hook removal easy. This is called "lipping" a bass. Be gentle and quick about lipping a bass and releasing it. But use a net in water where a snake or alligator or such might go after your submerged hand.

Bluegills and other freshwater panfishes have sharp spines in their dorsal and pectoral fins. So lift the fish from the water by the tippet, and then handle it *carefully* so you don't get poked by a spine. Or raise the fish by holding only the barbless fly (in forceps if you like) and then turn the hook's point down so the fish drops off into the water. Or use a net.

Landing species other than trout, the basses, and panfishes may require special techniques—pike and barracuda, for example, can bite off your finger if not handled properly. Know how to properly—and safely—land and manage the species you catch.

# UNHOOKING A FISH

A "barbless" hook has no barb at all behind its point, a "debarbed" (also sometimes called barbless) hook has had its barb smashed down with pliers. A barbed hook is always more difficult to remove from a fish than a hook with no barb or whose barb was smashed down, and a barbed hook can tear up fish's mouths. I've extracted fully barbed hooks from my own skin. I definitely did not like it. Trust me, you won't either. So I'm a fan of fully barbless hooks, and if I can't have them I'll settle for hooks whose barbs I've bent down with forceps or slim-jawed pliers.

To remove a large fly, such as a streamer, from a trout, just grasp the fly and back it out, opposite the direction it went in. It's hard to get a good grip on many flies because they're small. So grip smaller flies moderately in forceps and give them a quick push to free them.

### USING FORCEPS

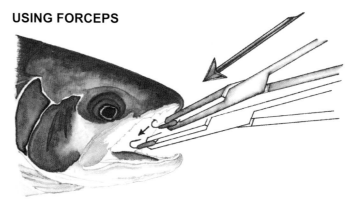

Other popular hook-removing tools feature a metal sleeve with an open slot for the tippet, or a coil of wire that allows the tippet to slip in. With these tools, you just slide the ring or little metal sleeve down the tippet to the fly and give the fly a quick push free.

### USING A HOOK-REMOVING TOOL

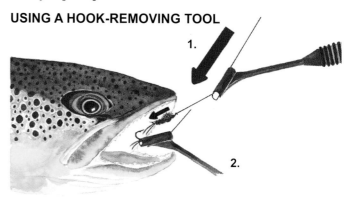

I carry both tools, as one or the other usually works best depending on how the fish is hooked. But if you aren't ready to buy both, start with forceps.

You'll be glad you have these tools when you fish for panfishes, as most have mouths too small for fingers to enter.

Largemouth and smallmouth bass possess wide jaws and normally take big flies, so with them fingers usually work better than tools for removing flies. Sometimes, however, forceps can help you work a bass fly free that's caught in tender gills or that's half-swallowed.

# CHAPTER 7

# Trout in Rivers

Fishing for trout in rivers has long been the most popular kind of fly fishing (long indeed—at least 300 years!). So it logically follows that this must be the *best* kind of fly fishing. But I don't think so. Yes, I'm fascinated by working a fly on or down in the currents of a trout river, but I'm also fascinated by working flies in or on smallmouth bass rivers and trout and largemouth bass lakes. Equal rewards, but different. And I love the differences too.

Actually, opinions abound as to just which fish and water represent fly fishing's Holy Grail. Some fly-fishers crave a steelhead river, others a tropical bonefish flat. Really, it's a matter of opinion—no one's right, but no one's wrong.

All this aside, trout rivers remain the standard and classic setting for fly fishing, and they're wonderful. Trout-river fishing also includes all those intriguing aquatic insects with their emergences from water to air, their flights and their mating, and the ways in which these activities move the trout to feed. And all those equally intriguing flies that imitate them.

For a river to be a *trout* river it must be cold—if the water's summer temperatures rise too high (around 70° and over), trout won't survive unless they can migrate to cooler water near springs or up tributaries. But a river too warm for trout may suit smallmouth bass. One blessing traded for another.

## TROUT SPECIES

The main four trout species are the rainbow, brown, cutthroat, and an almost-trout called the brook trout. Generally, the rainbow fights hardest, the brown is the smartest (followed closely by the rainbow), and the cutthroat and brook can turn fussy on the right day. They're all different in more subtle ways than these, and they're all magnificent.

**Rainbow**

**Brown**

**Cutthroat**

**Brook**

## TROUT-RIVER TYPES

### Creek

Size varies greatly among trout rivers. The smallest flowing trout water is a "creek," (also known as a brook or small stream), essentially a tiny river. Creeks typically hold small trout, but small trout are fun. (In fact, some creeks do hold large trout.) With few safe places to hide, creek trout are skittish and tend to require a quiet approach. The trees and high grasses along many creeks make casting a challenge. It's common on the smallest creeks to just reach out with the rod and *lower* the fly to the water; "dapping" we call it—no casting at all.

A creek.

### River

A typical trout river runs about 35 to 60 feet across in most places. But some rivers, such as Oregon's Lower Deschutes, are massive—too deep to ever wade across at

This is about as close to a classic trout river as you'll find—running clear and lively through forest and field, with pools, runs, riffles... A cast of modest length covers nearly all the good water. But don't limit yourself to classic trout rivers.

any point, even at their lowest flows, stunning in the sheer volume of water they push through second after second, and consequently, intimidating. But if you mentally break a big river down into its pockets, eddies, side-channels, and braided sections it begins to seem like a group of smaller rivers you can manage. And then there's the fact that most of the trout in big rivers lie within 10 or 20 feet of the bank. Don't be put off by big rivers. But do exercise even more caution than usual around them, especially when wading.

## Freestone River

"Freestone" is really just a fancy name for rivers that collect water straight off the surface—no man-made dams stall them and few, if any, springs feed them. Freestone rivers vary—they can meander through meadows or rush through boulders. In spring, warm days swell them with snow melt. In fall, they'll run dead low with the snow long gone after a long, dry summer. These extremes may leave the gravel bars they scour during high water exposed along their banks much of the year.

## Spring Creek

The term "spring creek" is misleading, because a "creek," as I said, is small. A spring creek may also be a trickle, but it can also be genuinely big water—size isn't the point. It's the source of the water that makes a spring creek a spring creek, and that source is springs. Spring creeks tend to run consistent in volume year round, so their banks grow right up to the edges, and their water is typically clear, rich, and almost steady in temperature. These are nearly ideal conditions for maximum capacity of trout and the creatures they feed upon. Many spring creeks do indeed carry heavy stocks of trout and insects. Those overfed trout in air-clear water may be especially wary, a real challenge for the fly fisher.

The Letort Spring Run is an historic Pennsylvania spring creek that, like all spring creeks, flows cold and constant year round. Decades ago it served as a laboratory for the historic development of fly designs and strategies for cautious trout.

## Tail-water

A "tail-water" trout river is fed from the base of a dam—the coldest water from the reservoir above. Some tailwaters meander like spring creeks, others crash through boulders, and yet others do both—tailwaters come in all sorts. Because their flows are controlled, tail-waters may rise and drop unnaturally.

Icy spring creeks and tail-waters, and rivers that start in the elevated cool of mountain valleys account for trout in unexpected places: Ohio, Oklahoma, Southern California, Alabama...

---

### JUST THE BASICS

**Here's a quick look at the nature of a trout river:**

- Trout rivers range from small (creeks) to massive.
- Most of the trout in big rivers lie close to the banks or in smaller features such as side channels or pockets.
- Freestone rivers gather from surface water, and range greatly in volume throughout the year. Spring creeks rise from springs and run at almost constant volume and temperature. Tailwater rivers emerge from dams and often rise and drop unnaturally.

---

## TACKLE FOR TROUT RIVERS

Here is a list of only those items you'll need specifically for fishing trout rivers. Certainly there is more you could carry, and use, but the following selection is a solid start. If you have questions about any of these items, refer back to chapter 1, "Equipment."

*Fly Line, Rod, Reel:* Just use the six-weight outfit with a floating line described in chapter 1, "Equipment." (You'll likely need a type-III sink-tip line on a second reel spool if you fish a streamer.)

*Leader and Tippet:* Two 7 1/2-foot 2X tapered leaders. One spool of 3X, one spool of 4X, one spool of 5X tippet (standard, not fluorocarbon). For a larger river, consider 9-foot 3X tapered leaders—your eventual standard.

*Strike Indicator:* Three, medium to large.

*Weight:* One container of lead-substitute split shot of various sizes.

*Fly Box:* One, large enough to contain the flies without crushing them.

*Eyeglasses:* One pair clear and one pair polarized sunglasses (both can be prescription or non. See chapter 1, "Equipment").

*Vest, Pack, or Box:* One vest (or chest or hip pack; forget a tackle box on a river).

*Net:* One. Hang it on the back of your vest (or the strap of your chest or hip pack) by a clip or retractor.

*Gadgets:* One pair of clippers for leader and tippet, one pair of forceps, one hook hone.

*Clothing:* See "Clothing" in chapter 1, "Equipment."

*Sunscreen:* Bring it, use it.

*Personal:* Bring water, food, a small first-aid kit, a small flashlight, and toilet paper.

*Waders:* One pair. Optional only on hot days.

*Wading Boots:* Required only if your waders aren't the boot-foot type. Studded (or felt, or studded felt) soles really help in rivers.

*Wading Staff:* Not required, but I strongly recommend one for ease and safety. See chapter 1, "Equipment" for options.

## Flies

A plain list of fly patterns for trout rivers makes perfect sense here...until you consider that a fly shop or even an online mail-order house can carry only a tiny percentage of the massive selections from all those fly companies. So, in the list that follows you'll see substitute patterns after each recommended fly pattern, making your search much easier—for example, if your local fly shop doesn't carry the Brooks' Sprout, just look at the substitute patterns and you'll see the X Caddis, which the shop does carry. Problem solved.

As you continue to fish rivers you will add flies that imitate specific insect hatches you keep encountering or patterns that for no clear reason consistently work. But, by starting out with only the list that follows you'll do fine; there will nearly always be a fly the fish will accept if you fish it well.

I recommend you get three of each pattern in each size. Flies get chewed apart by trout and broken off in trout and in snags all the time as a natural result of fishing. So, since there are 22 flies on the list (when you include the multiple sizes on some) you'll need to buy 66 flies in all. If the cost smarts too much, start with the bare-bones list on the following page, and get only two of each fly and size—the total price will be modest, and you can usually make do even with so few flies. But try to build up to the three-of-each-fly off the main list over time. (For more on flies, see Chapter 2, "Flies and Creatures They Imitate.") Here's your full list of flies for trout rivers.

## Imitative Nymphs

1. for mayflies (and small stoneflies): **Bead-Head Pheasant Tail** sizes 16, 14, 12 (Substitutes: Bead Head Gold Ribbed Hare's Ear, Ultimate Skip Nymph, A. P. Black Beaver or Peacock and Pheasant)

2. for caddis larvae and pupae: **Fox's Beaded Poopah, Olive** size 14 (Substitutes: Net Builder, Olive; Mercer's Z Wing Caddis, Olive; Pettis' Pulsating Caddis, Olive)

3. for big stoneflies: **Bitch Creek** (a metal bead for a head is optional) size 8 (Substitutes: Kaufmann Stone, Brown; Box Canyon Stone; Bird's Stonefly Nymph)

## Emergers

4. for mayflies and caddisflies: **Brooks' Sprout, *Callibaetis* or Mahogany** sizes 18, 16, 14 (Substitutes: X Caddis, Green; Morris Emerger, *Callibaetis*; Klinkhamer Special)

5. for midges: **Griffith's Gnat** size 20 (Substitutes: WD 40; Serendipity, Gray or Olive; Brooks' Sprout Midge, Black or Olive)

## Imitative Dry Flies

6. for mayflies: **Parachute Adams** (or "Adams Parachute") sizes 18, 16, 14, 12 (Substitutes: Compara-dun with a gray, tan, olive, or green body; Thorax Dun, *Callibaetis*; Adams)

7. for caddisflies (and small stoneflies): **Elk Hair Caddis** (original tan, or gray or green body) size 16, 14, 12 (Substitutes: Parachute Caddis with original tan, or gray or green body; Kings River Caddis; Goddard Caddis)

8. for big stoneflies (and big caddisflies): **Stimulator, Tan** (or Orange) size 8 (Substitutes: Improved Sofa Pillow; Rogue Foam Stone, Golden Stone; Madam X)

Bead-Head Pheasant Tail Nymph

Fox's Beaded Poopah (olive)

Bitch Creek

Brooks' Sprout (*Callibaetis*)

Griffith's Gnat

Parachute Adams

Elk Hair Caddis

Stimulator

Dave's Hopper

Copper John

Royal Wulff

Chernobyl Ant

Clouser Minnow

9. for terrestrials: **Dave's Hopper** (foam-body version is fine) size 10 (Substitutes: Letort Hopper, Parachute Hopper, Henry's Fork Hopper)

## Attractor Flies

10. nymph: **Copper John** size 14 (Substitutes: Gold Bead Prince Nymph; Gabriel's Trumpet, Gold; Rainbow Warrior)
11. medium-size dry fly: **Royal Wulff** size 12 (Substitutes: Royal Coachman Trude; Humpy, Yellow; Purple Haze)
12. big dry fly: **Chernobyl Ant** (any variation with a tan or yellow underside) size 8 (Substitutes: Parachute Madam X with an orange, red, yellow, or Royal body; Turck Tarantula; Madam X, Yellow)

## Streamer

13. for little fishes: **Clouser Minnow with olive back and white or yellow belly** (or brown back) size 6 (Substitutes: Marabou Muddler, Olive; Woolly Bugger, Olive; Morris Minnow, Brown, which is also called the "Skip's Brown Trout Minnow")

If you can't find one of these fly patterns or its substitutes at your local fly shop or online, ask a salesman to recommend something similar.

Once you fill this list, you'll be ready—no matter what mood the trout are in or what insect they're seeing on or in the water, you'll likely have at least one promising fly pattern to show them. And if you lose a fly that's working you'll have two identical back-up flies to take its place. Actually, you'll normally have several fly patterns the trout will take—trout are often open-minded about their feeding.

If you prefer to start out smaller (and cheaper) than the full list above, go with the short list below. This short list includes only fly patterns from the full list, so if you can't find a fly on the short list, check the full list for a substitute. The eight flies that follow will catch trout in rivers most of the time. If you go with the short list, I suggest you gradually add flies from the full list until you've collected them all. The short list is good, but the full list is better, and they both took me many hours of searching online and thumbing through catalogs (and, in fact, over forty years of tying and fishing trout flies) to compile—these are all excellent flies.

When you fish the limited selection below, keep an open mind about imitation—for example, the Griffith's Gnat was designed to suggest an emerging midge, but it could pass for a tiny emerging caddisfly or mayfly.

1. Bead Head Pheasant Tail (nymph) size 14
2. Bitch Creek, with or without a bead head, (nymph) size 8
3. Brooks' Sprout, *Callibaetis* or Mahogany, (emerger) size 14
4. Griffith's Gnat (emerger) size 20
5. Parachute Adams (dry fly) size 14
6. Elk Hair Caddis (original tan body or gray or green, dry fly) size 14
7. Stimulator, Tan (or Orange, dry fly), size 8
8. Clouser Minnow (olive back and white belly, or brown back and white belly, streamer) size 6

There—eight flies, coming to 24 flies with three of each pattern, and if you start out with only *two* of each pattern you'll have only 16 flies altogether for the price of dinner for two at a modest restaurant.

## TROUT-RIVER FEED

The better you understand the insects and other creatures trout in rivers eat, the more trout you're likely to catch. But believe me—you don't have to become an amateur "entomologist," someone who studies insects, in order to be an effective fly fisher. Even a little bug knowledge goes a long way. And it's genuinely interesting stuff.

Some of the insects and other creatures trout eat in rivers are different than the ones they eat in lakes; here are the ones you'll typically find in trout rivers: mayflies, caddisflies, stoneflies, midges, terrestrials, and small fishes.

Remember that observation (of the insects, the trout, the currents—everything) and a willingness to experiment (changing flies to something logical or illogical, fishing in places you've never tried) are at least as valuable to a fly fisher as a background in aquatic entomology.

For more on aquatic insects see chapter 2, "Flies and the Creatures They Imitate."

**Mayfly Nymph**

**Bead-Head Pheasant Tail**

## WADING

Wading is common practice in nearly all river fishing—not just for trout, but for smallmouth bass, steelhead, shad, Pacific and Atlantic salmon, and others, and for some kinds of saltwater fishing. The two main concerns in wading are (1.) avoiding a fall and (2.) staying safe if you do fall. You will fall, eventually, and you're wise to keep this in mind as you fish. And please read about courtesy in chapter 11 and about safety in chapter 14—both are important when wading.

### Here are the basics on wading:

1. You need wading boots (or bootfoot waders) that grip, for safety—felt-soles (if they're legal where you're fishing) or cleated waders or wading boots are excellent insurance against a fall. A wading staff maximizes that insurance.

2. Wade one foot at a time. That is, plant your left foot firmly, wiggle it a little to make sure it's secure, and *only then* move your right foot. Now make sure the right foot is secure before moving the left foot again, and so on.

3. Carry and *use* a wading staff—that third point of contact about quadruples your stability. Try to make a triangle with your feet and the staff's tip.

4. Wade sideways to the current—this provides the best stability and the least resistance to the flow.

5. Take your time. This allows you to look around and judge, see if the rocks are small or large, clean or slick with algae, and more. Slow wading is the safest wading.

6. Don't push it. If you feel uncomfortable going deeper— *don't* go deeper. At first, when your judgment lacks experience, you can really get yourself in trouble. Never risk your life for a fish.

7. Look downstream before wading out. If there's a nasty chute, rapid, canyon, falls, or anything else you don't want to be swept through (or over), don't wade upstream of this danger unless you're truly a safe distance from it.

8. With a fishing partner, locking arms or grasping one another's wrist is a real advantage in wading heavier water. Side by side, connected by one arm each, you're both far more stable than when wading individually. (Still, use a wading staff and don't tackle water that makes you nervous...)

9. Most falls happen in shallow water, the result of overconfidence and carelessness. So remember: while the pressure from current is usually weak in shallow water, the riverbed there is just as slick as anywhere else.

10. If you're wading without a wading staff, hold your arms straight out to your sides for better balance. Pointing your rod straight out from your body also helps.

11. When wading, as in all fishing activities, a friend nearby greatly increases your safety. This is true of about any outdoor sport: hiking, kayaking, swimming... Be wise and alert out there, fish with a friend, and wade safely out into those waters.

Making a triangle with feet and wading staff.

## FISHING THE DRY FLY OR EMERGER

Though fishing the dry fly was once widely acknowledged as the highest form of fly fishing, today it's generally considered the *easiest*. Sure, some dry-fly fishing is supremely challenging, but on the whole a floating fly casts with less fuss than a nymph rig or big streamer, and it's typically easier to work a floating fly up in plain sight than a sunken fly lost in the depths.

If trout are feeding at the surface of the water, "rising," a dry fly or emerger-fly makes sense on a river. If no trout are showing at the surface, a dry fly may still work fine, but this is normally the time for a nymph, or streamer.

A longish leader and tippet are the norm with a dry fly or floating emerger-fly. Trout feeding at the surface of the water are exposed to predators and know it—all that leader and tippet keep the alarmingly thick line well away from the fly and trout. Your starting dry-fly rig is shown in the illustration below.

### DRY-FLY AND EMERGER RIG

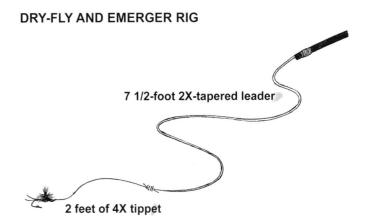

7 1/2-foot 2X-tapered leader

2 feet of 4X tippet

In very slow, clear rivers with difficult trout, a longer finer leader (9- to 12-foot 3X) and tippet (2 1/2 to 3 feet of 5X) might be better; and in rivers with easy trout, especially *big* easy trout, a heavier tippet (3X) might be wise. Still, the set-up in the illustration above will normally do the job. (You will probably come to prefer a 9-foot leader and longer tippet for most trout-river fishing, but that extra length would just cause you grief now.)

Before you begin fishing a dry fly or floating emerger-fly, work a small amount of fly floatant into the fly with your thumb and finger (unless you have a floatant other than a paste; if so, just follow its instructions). Keep the floatant spare to modest—too much can gum-up the fly's materials.

Dry-fly and emerger fishing on rivers is mainly about putting the fly quietly into the right place and allowing it to drift naturally with the current, as though there's no leader attached to it at all, "dead drift." You achieve dead drift by casting upstream, by making slack-line casts and mending (chapter 4, "Fly Casting"), and by using the two-foot (eventually, longer) tippet I recommend.

Occasionally, tugging a dry fly or emerger a little, either steadily or between pauses, is more effective than dead drift—usually because the insects on the water are lively or just because the trout are in a mood.

Normally, you want to fish a dry fly or floating emerger systematically, putting the fly out a little further (just a foot or two) after every couple of casts. After you've worked the fly out as far as makes sense, you wade upstream three or four feet and start over, casting the fly up but not far out, then further out, further... Follow this pattern until you've drifted the fly through all the promising water.

Throw the dry fly or emerger-fly upstream with a slack-line cast. While the currents are drawing out the curves (slack) in the line, leader, and tippet, the fly drifts freely. Sometimes trout are very discerning about fly drift, ignoring a dry fly or emerger-fly that drags unnaturally across the current even a little.

As the fly drifts towards you, pull in excess line—but not so much line that you cause the fly to drag. Mend the line as needed.

Casting the dry fly upstream isn't always best, or even possible. Suppose, for example, a trout is rising just above a fallen tree angling out into the current. An upstream cast (standing downstream) will catch the fly on a limb. So, you walk well up from the trout, cast downstream, feed out line, and watch the fly drift closer, closer...

Whenever the fly is on the water—watch it. When a trout takes it down in a splash or sip, raise the rod tip to set the hook.

When trout are taking insects on the river's surface, "rising," forget about searching likely water with your fly—you've found the trout. Pick a particular rising trout, or a group of them, and cast your fly so it drifts up to the trout's nose. Try to get the fly onto the water a few feet ahead of a rising fish so it won't land too close and frighten him off. Start low and work upstream from fish to fish.

When your floating fly grows sodden, a few quick casting strokes can snap out the moisture. If that fails, carefully squeeze the fly in a cotton cloth followed by a reapplication of floatant. Eventually, change flies.

## FISHING THE NYMPH

I'm convinced that river nymph fishing developed because fly-fishers grew tired of waiting for dry-fly action. Someone apparently figured out that trout do most of their feeding down near the riverbed.

From the trouts' perspective, feeding deep makes perfect sense—it's safer down there than up at the surface, and the riverbed is where the food lives. In relatively sterile rivers, where food is scarce, you may be able to draw a trout up to a dry fly about any time, hatch or no hatch. But in rivers heavy with aquatic life, trout usually need a good reason to expose themselves at the surface (except in the safety of low light). So if no mayflies are gliding on the currents and no grasshoppers are crashing onto the water, and no other floating or emerging creatures offer incentive, those well-fed trout will probably stay down in their riffles and runs among all those caddis larvae and mayfly nymphs. The nymph will be your best shot at hooking these fish.

Effective nymph fishing relies on a proper rig, which then gets adjusted throughout the day. The illustration below details such a rig. For very clear rivers, very slow rivers, picky trout, or all three, your leader and tippet might be longer and finer.

**NYMPH RIG**

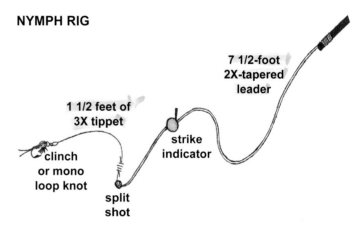

Here's how basic nymph fishing in rivers works—and it does work. Find a riffle or run or other promising trout water (we'll explore these next), step up next to it (but stay low if the water is clear and slow, or you'll spook the trout). If the water in front of you is too shallow for trout, wade out to about calf-deep. Judge the depth of the water (a rough guess is fine). Set the indicator up the leader from the fly 1 1/2 times (for slow to medium-fast currents) to *twice* (for fast currents) the depth. So if the water is three feet deep, set the indicator four and a half to six feet up the leader and tippet from the fly. Often, crimping a split shot or two onto the tippet, just above the knot connecting it to the leader, pays off (see the nymph-rig illustration above). Do not clamp your teeth on split shot to close them; use forceps.

Cast the whole rig upstream with a long, relaxed stroke—avoid the kind of quick, short casting stroke you'd use with a dry fly; it would snap the heavy nymph and indicator around and tangle them. Drop the rod-tip a little extra at the end of each forward and back casting stroke to widen the casting-loop and avoid tangles. Cast upstream, not far, 15 to 20 feet. Cast *out* only a little; the strike indicator, when it finally drifts near, should pass you only about two feet out from where you stand.

## FISHING THE NYMPH

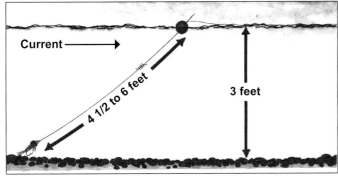

As the line drops at the end of your cast, lower your rod tip close to the water. The indicator will drift nearer and nearer; as it does, raise the rod to keep most of the slack line off the water (but not all of it—leave just a little loose line near the indicator). As the indicator drifts along naturally (like a dead-drift dry fly), continue to raise the rod-tip. Finally, your rod-arm is raised high, the rod up and angling slightly forward, to remove extra slack in the line. (Draw in a little line if you need to, so you can set the hook.)

As the indicator passes you, begin slowly lowering the rod's tip to feed line out. Continue lowering the rod until its tip nearly touches the water. When the indicator is straight downstream, start into another smooth, elongated cast with as few false casts as possible.

Throughout the long drift of the nymph, watch the indicator for even the slightest twitch or stall or dip, and when you see one, raise the rod tip *immediately* to set the hook. (My entomologist/fly-fishing-writer friend Rick Hafele recommends you strike once on *every* drift of the nymph, to get used to striking at the slightest sign from the indicator—great idea!) Your hook-set should be firm, but not violent.

Striking with a nymph varies. Essentially, the more stuff on the leader (strike indicator, split shot, weighted fly) the harder you need to strike to jerk the hook home. Same for depth—the deeper the fly, the harder the strike. So the range runs from light to *slightly* hard. Always, though, the nymph strike is *immediate.*

After each cast and drift of the nymph, or perhaps two drifts, cast the rig, upstream, about another foot further out. That's how it works, drifting the fly through the closest water out to the furthest, systematically, so your nymph drifts through all the good water.

When you've covered all the water near you, you take a few steps upstream and do it all again, working ever further out after each drift or two as before.

Once you've worked your way up through this particular piece of water systematically, you have a choice: if you were able to fish all the promising water, move upstream to the next spot; but if you didn't reach all the good water, you can walk back down to were you started, wade out further than the first time, and then work your way upstream again, your first casts dropping the fly just beyond the water you worked through before.

Another way is to start by covering all the water you can reach from one position, wading out and covering more water, and finally wading back to where you started, stepping upstream a bit, and then doing it all again.

Specifically during a caddisfly hatch, an effective approach can be to cast a weighted caddis-pupa fly out on a floating line upstream of the rising trout, and then let the fly swing slowly across the current, not far below the surface, like a swimming pupa.

## FISHING THE STREAMER

Working a streamer fly to imitate a small fish or fishlike creature is sometimes the most effective way to fish a trout river—it's also an excellent way to hook a big trout. Big-trout fishing tends to be slow, because big trout are generally few. For now, you'd be wise to concentrate on the nymph and dry fly. But keep streamer-fishing in the back of your mind and try it when the nymph and dry fly fail.

To fish a streamer, work the water systematically as you would with a dry fly or nymph, the big difference being that you'll work your way *downstream* rather than upstream. Rig up with a sink-tip line (the same WF 6 F/S type-III line

## STREAMER RIG

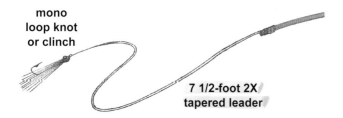

mono
loop knot
or clinch

7 1/2-foot 2X
tapered leader

described in chapter 9 for smallmouth bass) and a 7 1/2-foot 2X leader (you can skip a tippet if you like—in fact many fish a streamer on leaders only six feet long or shorter. If you want tippet, add 1 1/2 feet of 3X). With shallow or small streams a floating line may work best. See the illustration above.

Cast slightly upstream, let the line and fly sink—no retrieving—and then twitch the fly as it swings across the current, deep. You might even feed out some line if the current is quick, to keep the fly from swinging or rising too quickly. Mending line can help keep the fly from swinging in too soon.

When the fly is straight downstream, twitch and retrieve it until you have mostly just the sinking section of the line out of the rod, move downstream a couple of steps, and then cast up and well out again.

You won't cover all the water in strategic drifts as you would with a dry fly or nymph that follows a line of current, because the streamer is swinging *across* all the riverbed within reach. You just make a cast and swing or two, and then step downstream and do it again. Keep moving.

You'll feel the thump when a trout hits; just tug the hook home.

## FISHING A STREAMER

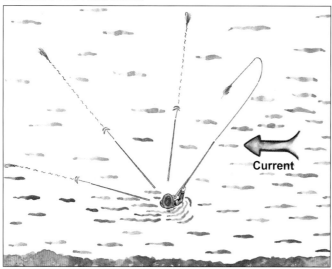

Current

## READING A TROUT RIVER

Much of the water in most rivers seldom if ever holds any trout worth your bother. So you need to know where good trout hold and where they feed.

The bottom line is that the trout want a place where (1.) they can be relatively safe, (2.) can hold comfortably in a modest flow, and (3.) are near a good current that provides food.

Considerable holding water for river trout falls neatly into the categories I'll describe, but a lot doesn't. Good holding water can come in all sorts of odd configurations. So first, learn to identify the classic lies. Later, open your mind and consider the three factors I mentioned above—safety, comfort, good current nearby—and if all three are present, fish through that water. Here are the classic river lies for trout.

## Riffle

A riffle is a fairly wide stretch of river typically about even in depth from bank to bank and carries a lively current. A riffle will run about two to four feet deep. Riffles may look unpromising, but in them are lots of edible insects, good current as protection from predators, and various depressions and boulders and such to break the current for a comfortable place to hold.

A riffle may be calm on its surface which means its bed is fairly even, a "smooth riffle," or churning around boulders scattered through its bed, a "broken riffle." Both kinds of riffles hold trout. (A broken riffle with many boulders that are large enough and exposed enough to create a slow, protected miniature pool of water behind each is really pocket water. Read on...)

Drift your nymph systematically through all the water you can comfortably reach. Riffles aren't usually dry-fly water, but sometimes...

## Run

Where a river gradually deepens and slows, lazing over large boulders on its bed, you have a run. Trout will lie among the boulders where you can lose a lot of nymphs—but also hook a lot of trout. Those trout may take a dry fly.

Think of a run as a slower, deeper version of a riffle. Many runs feed into pools, some stand by themselves.

# Pool

Even non-anglers recognize a pool—a near-pond with a bouncing current flowing into its top, slowing finally to almost still water through its deep center, the water shallowing and picking up speed to pour over the wide thin edge at the lower end of the pool. (The top of a pool may be a run.)

A pool has a "head" where the water comes in; a "body" which is its slow, deep center; and a "tail," where the water leaves the pool. The edge of the tail, where the water breaks, is the "lip."

Trout particularly hold and feed along the long triangle of current that slows and dies in the body of the pool: the "current tongue."

Trout will also hold here and there around a pool, especially where there's a little current, and will sometimes feed down near the shallow lip at the tail of the pool, often due to a hatch of insects.

# Pocket Water

A sort of riffle strewn with big, exposed boulders is what fly-fishers call "pocket water." The deeper water behind each boulder is a miniature pool, and you fish each pocket as though it were a pool. Pocket water is often overlooked by fly-fishers, making it all the more promising.

# Bank

Where a river turns, its outside edge may run deep right up against the bank and such a spot is simply called a "bank." Trout will hold in the good current and depth of bank water and take a nymph or dry fly or streamer.

An "undercut bank" has been scoured back underneath by the current, leaving an excellent trout lie.

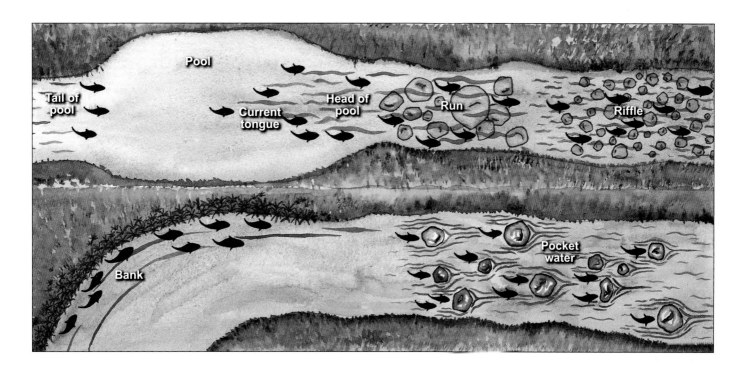

## Other Lies

I watch for a feature I call a "slot." Where a river bends a little, leaning its current to one side, there is often a long, narrow, deepish depression that can hold trout. The water across from a slot is often nearly still and seldom holds trout. Slots aren't common, but they're around.

An "eddy" or "back eddy" is a small to big, slowly rotating current—a circle or oval of flow—where trout love to rise (see page 61).

Another excellent area for trout rising can be a thread of slow current between a bank and good current. White foam and debris—and insects—collect there, hence its nicknames "foam line" and "scum line."

Trout in the lazy water of spring creeks, meadow rivers, and some tail-waters may lie wherever they can find safety, usually in the depths, close to deep water next to the bank, or among water plants. Pools and riffles and such may simply not exist. So try your nymph wherever a trout might hold and hope for an insect hatch to bring trout out to rise in the open so that you can fish a dry fly or emerger.

---

# A DAY ON A TROUT RIVER

*It's one thing to read about fishing and another to actually go out and do it. So let's apply what you've learned about casting and rigging and the rest to a day on a trout river—you're going fly fishing! (Well...in print, anyway.)*

You look upstream and downstream to see where the river stalls in pools, rushes through rapids, sweeps through riffles, and jostles through pocket-water. The riffle upstream is just a longish cast from bank to bank, making this about a medium-size trout river. A narrow pool in shadow, mottled where the low morning sun pierces the forest, lies before you. You do the wise thing: you wait, and watch.

In the soft edge of your vision your fishing partner crosses the river just below the shallow lip of the pool so he can fish up the far side. Before you a mayfly flitting through a shaft of light passes a caddisfly fluttering nervously over the water. Not much to see. Until the quiet rise of a trout appears upstream along your bank, well in from the current tongue of the long pool. You wait for the fish to rise again. Finally, it does. Nothing appears to be hatching—watching the smooth surface of the clear water reveals no emerging insects of any kind, and no caddis or mayflies or even midges stand riding the currents. But there are specks here and there on the water, and finally you see that they are crumpled, failed insects. It's a mix: mayfly spinners, some midges still half trapped in the shucks that finally doomed them, other things with legs and perhaps wings. You decide to just try something plausible and small, subtle. So you tie 5X tippet to your leader and a size-16 Brooks' Sprout onto the tippet—5X seems light enough for this quiet trout in such quiet water.

After two careful practice casts, to judge the distance, the fly is drifting to the fish. It passes him, and he rises. Three more presentations and he takes it. Soon you draw him over the lip of your net. That's one clean twelve-inch brown trout and a good start for your day. But after watching carefully for more risers, you see none and decide to change tactics.

It's mid-July—terrestrial season—and the patch of tall, pale grass stretching up your bank of the pool suggests a grasshopper fly. But it's too early in the day for that. You give the Sprout another 15 fruitless minutes. It's time, you decide, for a nymph. You could nymph fish the pool, but you want to see what's up the river. So you walk upstream to the riffle, wade into the shallows, roll up a sleeve, reach down into the cool current and stretch your fingertips around a flattened stone. Up close, in the air, the smooth underside reveals a few small scurrying mayfly nymphs, dark and leggy. But three substantial green worms cling there: caddis larvae. You return the stone, slide a corkie strike-indicator up your leader, tie on 3X tippet, and then tie on a size-14 Pettis' Pulsating Caddis Pupa, Olive. It's really a pupa-imitation, but it's close to the color and size of the three larvae, and not far from the right shape. Drifted along the bottom like a larva swept into the current it will look just fine.

But it's a small fly, and too light by itself for this quick water. You crimp a No. 1 split shot on right above the knot connecting tippet to leader.

You step quietly out a little further into the edge of the smooth riffle, just far enough out to reach the closest water carrying real flow and depth. Looks about two feet deep out there, and swift, so you set the indicator three feet up the leader and tippet from the fly.

You make the kind of drawn-out, wide-loop cast that keeps the fly and indicator apart, and try to make it smooth, all for insurance against a tangle. The rig drops upstream and a little out. Now, *nothing* will draw your attention from that strike indicator. You take up the slack line by raising the rod as the indicator comes near. Right in front of you it shivers. You immediately give a light tug and feel nothing, so you just let the indicator drift on past you as you lower the rod to feed out line. After a second cast and drift through the same line of current, you cast out another foot. Then the indicator *really* dives and you strike. Your heart soars at the resistance, but it's...leaden. You've snagged a rock. You tug lightly a couple of times but the fly stays snagged. So you wade upstream a few feet—quietly, so as not to alarm fish—reach the rod upstream and low, and tug again. You feel the line give as the fly comes free of the rocks, opposite of the way it went in. Such tactics—tugging the fly upstream, pulling from various angles, letting the line go slack between tugs, even kicking at the rocks where the fly is stuck—sometimes work. But often the only solution is to just point the rod at the fly, pull hard until the tippet breaks, and tie on a new fly. Losing nymphs, you well know, just goes with fishing them effectively.

You check the hook's point, and then return to the pattern: cast, drift the nymph through, pick up, cast a little further out... The indicator dives again, and the urge sweeps over you to ignore it, to just write this off as another rock—but you know better than to guess at rocks, and set the hook to feel the eruption of a trout in panic. He runs hard, stealing line, then backing. Good fish. You let him run, and when he leaps you drop the rod-tip briefly. This *really* is a good fish, for this river anyway. When the battle is over, you slide an 18-inch rainbow trout, pink-banded and crisply spotted, over the lip of your net. You keep the fish in the water as you back the fly out (easy to do with its smashed-down barb). You cradle the fish, careful not to squeeze it even for moment, until it starts to work against the current and finally swims out of your hands. Already your day is practically made.

You work methodically upstream through the riffle, covering all the good water you can reach. Finally at the top of the riffle, you walk back down to where you started and then wade out further than before to reach the deeper water past the riffle's center. Resetting the indicator about six feet up from the fly seems right for the roughly 3 1/2-foot depth. But after a few casts with the fly seeming never to bump the bottom, you pinch a second split shot on just above the first one. That does it. You hook and land a 10-inch brown and then a 14-inch rainbow. You lose another fish so quickly that you can't even guess its size. You spend most of the next hour working the long riffle, landing and releasing a few fish. You snagged two more times and the second time had to break off the fly. Such is nymphing.

Now at the top of the riffle, ready to move on, you sense the last trace of morning's coolness relent under the high sun. Upstream, your partner pulls off his jacket to stuff it in the pouch in the back of his vest. A run stretches upstream, a stand-alone run deepening through its head into an easy flow through a near constant and considerable depth, and then shallowing, rather than dying in the dark stillness of a pool. You watch the tail of the run a while. There might be trout rising there, taking hatching mayflies or caddisflies or even tiny midges. Nope.

So the nymph still makes sense with no action at the water's surface, but a Royal Wulff, green-and-red-banded and bristling with hackle, seems right, something to give the trout a little excitement. You change to 4X tippet. The 3X tippet you coil up and tuck into a vest pocket. You try the shallows first. Nothing. Then on an S cast you throw the bushy Coachman up and a little out where the water deepens. Each cast that follows puts the fly further out. When you've reached nearly to the center of the run you see the dark shape of a trout forming as it glides up through the kaleidoscopic flow. Now it's suspended over varying green depths just downstream of the drifting fly. You wait, your insides trembling with anticipation. Then the trout seems to kiss the fly. You raise the rod and two pounds of angry rainbow trout plunge hard and then come racing back up to spring from the water.

The Coachman brings no more action over the next fifteen minutes through some promising water. A nymph? Maybe... Or something *really* bizarre? You take out the 3X tippet and tie it on again, and on the 3X, a big Chernobyl Ant. Near the head of the run, where the water is thinner, you throw out the rubbery fly to watch it drift. It's large enough that you can see its legs, clear out there, bending to the current. The fly spins slowly in some swirling water. A head slams it down. Several minutes later you think, That's one fine brown, as you free the fish in the shallows.

Over the next hour you toss that goofy fly out again and again to bounce absurdly on the current, and here and there—once over a deep slot along a bank, once alongside a choppy current tongue in a pool, and twice behind boulders in pocket water—a good fish accepts the fly in a patient rise or snatches it in a rush.

Something makes you glance upstream. It's a grasshopper flying laboriously over a grass-bordered run. You watch as it splats down. It seems to twitch, probably snapping its great kicking legs in vain. Then it goes down in a white, murderous slash. You cut off the Chernobyl and replace it with a Dave's Hopper, rub on some floatant. With such a big dry fly you might as well stick with the 3X tippet.

You work up the run, smacking down the big fly along the bank. Three trout, one a real dandy, come to net.

---

By the time you and your friend return from a long dinner break in town, it's getting late. That first long pool you fished seemed filled with promise for the dry fly. Such water, you know, is often at its best during the evening rise. Now you're standing well back from the pool as you watch the dark water. The last arc of the sun throws its final rays from the hilltops, none touching the pool. You see a workmanlike rise. You come closer, crouching low. Two more rises appear in two other places from other fish. At the water's edge you notice caddisflies skittering on the current. One goes down hard. A caddis flies by and you catch it. In your palm it's got some size, its body is green, and its wings are spotted gray. You tie on the 4X tippet and to that a size-14 Elk Hair Caddis, and add floatant. The trout continue their feeding. You walk to the tail of the pool and work out some line. Above the murmur of the current you hear a caddis go down in a splash upstream, somewhere in the charcoal-colored shadows.

# CHAPTER 8

# Largemouth Bass and Bluegills in Lakes

You'll find largemouth bass in every American state except Alaska, and in Canada all along its 3,000-mile border with the US. In Mexico and South America too. Therefore, you probably live near largemouth water, and that's a gift.

The largemouth bass is a first-class game fish that, when hooked, will strain a stout tippet and leap up to slap the top of the water with his tail. He's easy if naive, but if he's been caught before he can test a seasoned fly fisher's skill. And largemouth-bass flies are colorful, sometimes a bit crazy, and simply fascinating.

Though largemouth and smallmouth bass may share the same fresh water and confuse you at first with their resemblance to one another, they really are very different fishes. Largemouths like lily pads and reeds and fallen timber and often nestle themselves back into them. Smallmouths will haunt water-plants and boulders and gravel and rocky ledges. Largemouths will tolerate only slow currents and generally avoid them altogether while smallmouths love a rushing river. Largemouths will eat big insects but prefer bigger things like frogs and small snakes and even small birds; smallmouths eat some large things, but often take the same little insects on which trout make a living. Largemouths fight hard and briefly with a whole bag of dirty tricks they're happy to open while smallmouths also fight hard but for about as long as you let them. These fishes are different enough that you could be an excellent smallmouth angler and fail with largemouth, and vice versa—but you won't fail with either fish if I have something to say about it. Which, of course, I do.

## IDENTIFYING LARGEMOUTH BASS

A typical largemouth bass is dark- to light-green along its back and a lighter green along its flanks with a dark smudgy horizontal stripe running along each flank from its head back to its tail. A typical smallmouth bass is yellowish brown overall with a row of dark *vertical* stripes down each flank. Both fishes have pale bellies. So there are differences, but obviously these fishes look similar. The easy test is the mouth—if it (including its bony rim) reaches back further than directly below the eye, it's a largemouth, if it reaches no further back than the eye it's a smallmouth bass.

An average largemouth might run 12 inches and a pound in weight. But two-pounders are common and there are five-, six-, and eight-pounders out there. Ten pounds or over is a trophy largemouth *anywhere.*

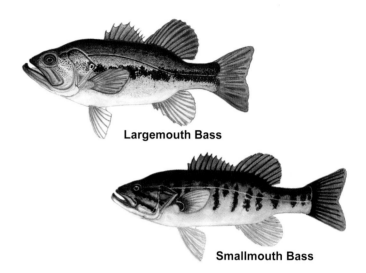

**Largemouth Bass**

**Smallmouth Bass**

## PANFISHES

There are several common panfishes, and most prefer the same standing water and lily pads and logs that largemouths like. Most panfishes also prefer largemouths' ideal water-temperature range. Here are a few panfishes you're likely to find with largemouths: black crappie (pronounced "crop-pea"), redear sunfish, green sunfish, rock bass, white crappie (see chapter 12, "Other Fishes"), and that's still not all of them. But the panfish you'll find most consistently alongside the largemouth bass, from the Deep South to the Canadian border and north, from the Pacific Coast across North America to the East Coast, is the bluegill. So we'll concentrate on the bluegill here.

The bluegill is slim when viewed from the top, and a plump oval when viewed from the side. A bluegill's cheeks (gill covers) are edged with powder-blue and there's a black tab on the rear of each. The bluegill looks similar to the redear sunfish and some other panfishes that, like the bluegill, often hang around the weeds and docks at the edges of a lake—but

**Largemouth bass**

**Bluegill**

if you hook a roundish panfish that pulls like a tiny tractor, who cares if it's a bluegill or a green sunfish or a pumpkinseed?

A good bluegill might be six inches long and around three ounces—but you can always hope for one of those 10-inch leviathans that presses the scale down towards a pound. A two-pounder is...breathtaking.

Bluegills are easy to catch when gathered to spawn in spring but can get tough later in the season on hard-fished water. Still, in their usual abundance there always seem to be plenty of takers among them. When bass won't be caught, bass anglers are often thankful for bluegills.

## LARGEMOUTH BASS AND BLUEGILL WATERS

### Farm Pond

The classic small water for largemouth bass and panfish is the man-made farm pond. Such ponds are good for beginners because everything is close and easy to sort out. There are other kinds of ponds, though, that can be just as good—the abandoned quarry pond and the natural pond, among others.

### Natural Lake

Natural lakes run from almost pond-small to vast. Natural lakes tend to hold their volume well, though there may be a big difference between their water levels in spring and fall.

## TACKLE FOR LARGEMOUTH AND BLUEGILLS

Here is a list of only the gear and such you'll need specifically for largemouth bass and bluegills in lakes, reservoirs, and ponds. You could easily add to this list, but you'll do fine with

### Reservoir

A reservoir is created by a dam, which backs up a stream or blocks the drainage of a gully or valley. Reservoirs can be any size, from tiny to massive. If their water is released for agriculture or generating electricity, reservoirs may fluctuate greatly in volume. This is a reservoir of several thousand acres in Arkansas.

what's here. If you have questions about any of these items, refer back to chapter 1, "Equipment."

*Fly Line, Rod, Reel:* Use the six-weight outfit described in chapter 1 with just the floating line (not the full-sinking or sink-tip lines).

*Leader and Tippet:* For largemouth bass: two 7 1/2-foot 0X tapered leaders. One spool of standard 1X tippet. For bluegills: two 7 1/2-foot 2X tapered leaders. One spool standard 3X tippet (the 3X is for when a large bass grabs your bluegill fly, but you can go to 4X or even 5X tippet for bluegills that are persnickety).

*Fly Box:* One, large enough to contain the bass flies without crushing them.

*Eyeglasses:* One pair clear glasses and one pair polarized sunglasses (both can be prescription or non).

*Vest, Pack, or Box:* One vest (or chest or hip pack or tackle box. I prefer a tackle box in a boat, but nowhere else).

*Gadgets:* One pair of clippers, one pair of forceps, one hook hone.

*Clothing:* See "Clothing" in chapter 1, "Equipment."

*Sunscreen:* Bring it and use it.

*Personal:* Bring water, food, a first-aid kit, a small flashlight, and toilet paper.

*Watercraft:* You may be able to find good bluegill fishing from shore or a dock because bluegill tend to mill around an area. But largemouth bass spread out and move around, so you'll need a float tube or inflatable kick boat or boat of some kind for them. As I mentioned in chapter 1, "Equipment"— do not go into dangerous water (snakes, alligators, current) in a float tube or kick boat.

*Life Vest:* Always with a boat, often with an inflatable float tube or kick boat or such (check state law). Safety...

*Waders:* For a float tube or kick boat, one pair. None with a boat.

*Fins:* One pair for a float tube or fin-powered (rather than oar-powered) kick boat. None for a boat.

*Anchor:* Optional, but handy, one for now (two are ideal for a boat).

Zonker · Woolly Bugger, White · bass bug

Dahlberg Diver · Copper John · sponge spider · popper

## Flies

The topic of fly patterns for almost any fish is vast, largemouth bass and bluegills included—take it from a guy who's published nine books on tying flies. So as you continue to fish for largemouths and bluegills you will add flies that imitate specific creatures *your* largemouths and bluegills eat, or flies that are known killers in your area, or that you just try and your fish like. Nevertheless, the list that follows will nearly always provide a fly that will work.

Flies get chewed up, snapped off, and their hook-points broken as a natural result of being fished—so I recommend you get three of each pattern, a total of 21 flies. (For more on flies, see chapter 2, "Flies and the Creatures They Imitate.")

## Underwater Flies for Largemouth Bass

1. For imitating small fishes: **Zonker, Olive or Natural** size 4. (Substitutes: Double Bunny, Olive; Clouser Minnow, Olive or Brown; Marabou Muddler, Olive or Brown and with or without a metal bead or cone.)
2. For general use: **Woolly Bugger, White, with a bead or cone**, size 6. (Not my favorite streamer for largemouth, but a reliable one and easy to obtain. I actually prefer the substitutes. Substitutes: Scorpion [Whitlock's], White [only comes in size 4, which is fine]; Bouface, Olive; Morris Minnow, Brown [also called "Skip's Brown Trout Minnow"], which comes only in size 4, and that's fine too.)

## Floating Flies for Largemouth Bass

3. For general use: **a hair bass bug, brown or yellow or tan or green (preferably with a white or yellow face)** with a *body* (not including the tail) about 5/8-inch long (not over 3/4-inch long. Bass-bug hook sizes are wildly inconsistent, so body-length is the best gauge). That's small as largemouth flies go, but with a bug this size you can hook and land any decent bass—not just the big ones. Get a bug with a monofilament-loop snag guard. (Substitutes: cork popper, Messinger Frog, foam popper.)

4. Diving fly: **Dahlberg Diver in white or yellow or purple** with a body (including the trimmed-hair diving-collar but not including the tail) about 5/8-inch long (not over 3/4-inch, same reason explained above for the hair bug). Should include a monofilament snag-guard. (Substitutes: Umpqua Swimming Frog; any hair or foam diving bug in white, yellow, or tan [a diving bug has a head or body tapering from narrow in front to broad at the rear].)

## Flies for Bluegills (and other panfishes)

5. A general sinking fly: **Copper John** size 12. (Substitutes: Bead Head Gold Ribbed Hare's Ear; Gabriel's Trumpet, Gold; or any bead-head or well-weighted nymph.)
6. A subtle floating fly: **sponge spider, yellow or white** size 12. (Substitutes: any standard dry fly—such as the Parachute Adams, Royal Wulff, Elk Hair Caddis...)
7. A general popper: **a cork or foam popper, overall yellow, white, or chartreuse** size 10 (many companies make such bugs, so they're widely available).

## Fence Riding

With a fly of a certain size you can treat water containing both largemouth bass and panfishes as your personal roulette table, each cast a roll of the dice. Your next strike could come from a two-pound bass or a seven-inch bluegill or a pound-and-a-half crappie or a green sunfish...

In his book *The Sunfishes*, author Jack Ellis offers a fly called the Fence Rider, basically a little hair bass bug, that is tied always on a size-6 Mustad 3366 hook. Ellis explains that the fly is small enough that big bluegills can take it in but large enough to attract and hold substantial largemouth. I've been following Jack's fence-riding formula for years now, and having a blast!

But when you buy a fly, how do you know if it's tied on a Mustad 3366? You don't. So I measured a size-6 Mustad 3366 and found it was about 7/8-inch in total length, from the rear edge of the bend to the tip of the looped end called the eye. Therefore, if you want to do some fence riding, buy some floating hair, foam, or cork bugs on a hook of this length. Go ahead—bring your ruler to the fly shop.

# FISHING A BASS BUG OR POPPER

This is the most reliable process I've found for working a floating hair bug or popper (or a diving bug, which I'd make dive some) for both largemouths and bluegills:

1. Cast the bug to plop down within *inches* of cover (a fallen tree, lily pads...).
2. Right away, give the bug one or two quick jerks by snapping the rod's tip *low* and to the *side*. The snaps are short, so the bug lurches with a light chug (not a loud pop that would scare the bass) but as soon as the rod-tip has jerked the bug, flick the tip immediately back to where it started, so the bug isn't dragged away from the cover.
3. Let the bug lie *motionless* until the circular wavelets of its movement expand over the water and die—this takes a little while (at least 10 to 15 seconds, on the watch).
4. Give the bug a *slight* draw, just enough to make its head dip a little, and no more.
5. Let the bug lie motionless for five to ten seconds; then start it swimming towards you, slowly at first, and then ever faster, drawing in line.
6. When the bug is mostly back to you, pick it up and cast it out to the next spot, usually two or three feet down the shoreline from the last spot.

A bass can slam or gently mouth the bug any time during this entire sequence—I've had plenty of bass shoot up to catch the bug in midair, so even if the fly is only *near* the water, watch, and stay sharp.

Set the hook hard with largemouths, harder yet with largemouths and snag-guard flies.

## FISHING A SINKING FLY

Simple: if the bass and bluegills won't come up to a floating fly, try a diver (fish it about as I've described for a hair bug, but use long draws sometimes to make it swim under water). If they won't take a diver, toss a sinking fly (Zonker, Woolly Bugger...) out around the cover. Use your full-floating line. Let the fly sink for a few seconds with no retrieve; then strip it in slowly (the strip retrieve), in jerks and pauses; set the hook if you feel any resistance or see the line tighten or the leader twitch. Holding the rod's *tip* down *on* the water and pointing the rod straight down the line will help you feel a take of the fly. Set the hook hard.

## READING A BASS-BLUEGILL LAKE

Largemouth bass and bluegills will sometimes hold deep, particularly through icy winter and during the sweltering middays of summer, but sometimes just because they're in a mood. These fishes can be caught in deep water on a fly—I've done it many times. But fishing a fly deeper than, say, 10 feet for largemouth bass is tricky. It requires that you understand the deep structure bass seek and can find that structure in your water. That, in turn, requires a sonar machine called a "fish finder" or a topographical map of the lake's bed or specific local knowledge or just lots of time

on that water—and none of these is easy to come by for a beginning fly fisher. So for now, forget deep water.

Fortunately, bass and bluegills (and some other panfishes) spend lots of time in or near the shallows, where you can see the cover they like. So the shallow water, from around one and a half to ten feet deep, is where you'll begin your fly fishing for these species. And you'll still be fishing there for them a decade from now—the shallows are always an excellent place to seek bluegills and largemouth bass.

### Hard Cover

Long ago I coined the term "hard cover" to describe objects in a lake that provide largemouth bass and bluegills solid shelter, the kind of shelter flying predators can't penetrate. These include fallen and floating logs, the roots of cypress trees, moored boats, docks, old pilings, and such. Bass may favor hard cover, but bluegills seem equally at home in about any kind of cover, hard or otherwise.

### Water Plants

Lily pads and bulrushes, milfoil and other water plants around a lake's shoreline are "soft cover" for bass and bluegills. Throw your fly in close to these water plants and if there are openings and channels in them, try your fly in there too—and then thank God for snag-guards.

## Weather

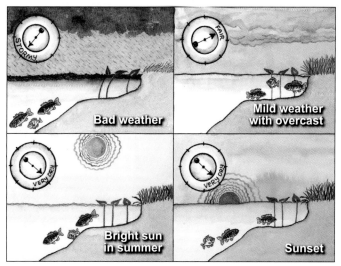

## The Seasons

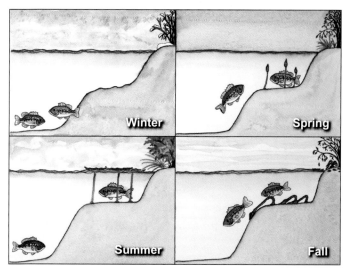

A dropping barometer—which accompanies souring weather—often sends bass and bluegills deep. But cloud cover on a mild day can punch up the action even in sizzling midsummer. The *start* of a big weather change, for better or worse, may put bass and bluegills on a feeding binge. Bright sun can drive bass deep during the day, but they'll go shallower in morning and evening.

Bass and bluegills will hold in water from only a foot deep down to twenty feet or deeper, typically, close to the lake's bed. Through icy winter bass and bluegills will stay deep, but as the water warms in spring they'll move ever shallower and increasingly visit the shallows, mostly around sunrise and sunset. The cooling air and water of autumn will invigorate bass and bluegills, but eventually send them ever deeper.

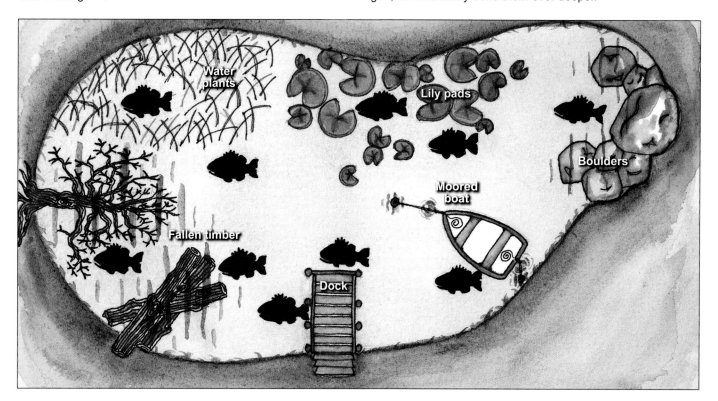

## A DAY ON A LARGEMOUTH BASS AND BLUEGILL LAKE

A small round lake lies calm before you in the hazy morning sunlight. Your friend is already headed across the lake in his float tube. Summer's bristling heat has been filling the afternoon air lately, so you know that morning and evening will probably provide your best fishing. Therefore, time is precious and though you ache to toss out a fly, wisely, you sacrifice a full minute to look carefully around.

On the far side of the lake a man sits in a rowboat, just out from shore. He seems settled, probably watching a bobber and hoping to hook a catfish or crappie. He won't likely bother your shoreline.

A splash well off to your right makes you step out onto a flat rock in the shallows to see what happened. Over the green-matted bottom, next to a little patch of lily pads, mill a few dark elongated shapes, probably bluegills. You lean out, looking to where you heard the splash, and see dying ripples in a patch of open water among the pads; perhaps a bass that attacked something? Excellent! Already two good signs that the bass and bluegills are shallow and active.

You keep watching. A dragonfly soars near, hovers, alights briefly on tall grass, and then soars away. In the clear shallows of the boat launch you notice the bluegills gathering over the gravel to watch you in fascination.

Nothing else of note happens or appears. So you drag your little boat into the edge of the water and set it up. You rig your rod, and tie a hair bass bug onto stout tippet—the bluegills are tempting, but you really want to try for bass in the promising remainder of morning before moving on to smaller game.

You climb in, row out, and then halt the boat with a nudge of the oars. It just occurred to you that that patch of lily pads next to the boat launch might be worth a cast—it's just the kind of cover most anglers would pass up while imagining how good the fishing must be clear across the lake. A common mistake. You drop your bug along the edge of a pad.

You make the fly sputter, then rest. It twitches nervously. You almost set the hook, but hesitate. A few more casts bring nothing. You row in to see two good bluegills holding in a shaft of sunlight alongside the pads. That explains the twitching bug—even a big bluegill will never get its little mouth around this hook. Besides, you're in the mood for bass.

So you row out a bit and stop the boat. You toss your bug back where you heard the splash earlier, near shore among lily pads. After a gurgling lurch the bug rests quietly a while. Then you give it a tiny tug—a bass slams the fly, sending up spray. You grip the line and jerk the rod back hard to drive the hook in past the mono snag guard. The bass shakes up on his tail and then heads for the pads. He's too strong, you can't stop him. Then your taut line points at a cluster of lily pads crushed together like banded parsley in a grocery store. The bass encircled the stalks with tippet and pulled it tight.

You tighten the line, which coaxes your boat up to the pads. The bass gives the pads an angry shake. You can see him now, and he's a good one. You reach down, and then hoist a two-pound largemouth by the jaw. You unhook the fish, lower him to the water, watch him swim away. You can do that here—there are no cottonmouths, alligators, or such. If there were, you'd be more careful, probably use a net to bring in and release each fish.

Fifty more feet of shoreline brings nothing, and then another bass takes your bug alongside a dock in front of a neat green lawn and clean white house. The bass is a ten-incher—in other words, big enough to be fun. Soon after, a bass of around two pounds quietly sucks down the bug next to a fallen log, explodes up when you snap the hook home, and shakes off the bug with somersaults in the air.

The next hundred or so feet of shoreline is quiet. You notice the high sun and your felt shirt clinging to your perspiring shoulders. You strip off the heavy shirt leaving only the lightweight fabric of the real summer shirt with its long sleeves to protect you from sunshine. You clip off the bug and tie on a Dahlberg Diver—perhaps the bass are still there but unwilling to show themselves at the now dazzling surface. You toss the Dahlberg down a slot in a patch of lily pads. You give the fly a tug, let it sit, and then draw and twitch it so that it glides and flips its tail a few inches down—that's when the bass hits. You wrestle the fish and soon raise a 1 1/2-pounder by the jaw. Then you unhook and gently release the fish.

Two more bass hit the diving fly in almost the same spot, a squarish corner of the lake. It looked so good here, you had to give it some extra time. After the second fish, though, the action ends.

It's noon, and the glaring sun pours down heat onto your shoulders. No bass will like this—that last dead half hour left little doubt. So you add a couple of feet of lighter 3X tippet to your 1X tippet—but that's as light as you want to go, since a good bass could grab your little bluegill fly at any time. You tie on a little cork panfish bug and begin to work it just as you would for bass. Soon you see something pick at the popper but not take it down. A little later you twitch the bug and see the boils of fleeing bluegills around it. They're not having it—time for stealth. You tie on a yellow sponge spider.

A little canal stretching back between two mats of milfoil, under the long and shaggy limb of a shoreline tree, looks just right. You toss the spider in there with a low cast and work it gently, just enough to make the supple legs shudder. A big bluegill rolls on the fly. You set the hook, and remember just how hard a round bluegill can pull. Your six-weight rod bends deep into its stout butt section.

You know that bluegills tend to group, so you keep fishing the canal, hook two slightly smaller bluegills, then nothing.

You find a bluegill here and there along the next hundred feet of shoreline, and finally a bunch of them too small even to take the little spider. Now the bluegills aren't liking this high sunshine any more than the bass did, and neither are you. You head back to meet your friend at the boat launch and drive into town for a very late lunch.

---

It's four in the afternoon when you return. You watch your friend rock and bob away to your right in his float tube. To your left you see shoreline in shadow. You row there. The last hours turn out just as good as you'd hoped. The bass are feeding, though they won't come up. So you hook several by letting a Conehead Woolly Bugger sink straight down along the outer edges of the weed beds and around docks, and then working it back slowly, in little tugs.

As the sun sets you can't resist the smacking of bluegills feeding on top. You add the lighter tippet to your 1X again and try the cork popper—splat, chug-chug, long pause, dip, pause...the same sequence you used for the bass—and catch lots of bluegills, even a couple of stout crappies.

Finally, in the near-dark, you find that a steady series of gentle tugs on a hair bug moves the bass that seemed to have entered the shallows in an invisible wave. You land half a dozen—one probably three pounds—and then head for the boat launch in the quiet of evening, the spiky silhouette of the tree tops against an iron-gray sky still tinted blue to the west.

# CHAPTER 9

# Smallmouth Bass in Rivers

In the Pacific Northwest, if it's not a trout, a salmon, or a mythical steelhead, it doesn't count for much...if it counts at all. That's the general view among fly-fishers around here, but I don't share it—for example, I consider the smallmouth bass a first-class sport fish. He can hit with a wallop and then thrash and run long after your eyebrows have risen with respect. And he can be crafty. Sure, if a smallmouth's isolated from the angler's tricks he'll be a pushover—just like a sheltered trout—but the more he's pestered with lures and flies the more cautious he'll grow. Hook and release him once or twice and he'll turn downright contemplative. I have nothing but admiration for trout, salmon, and steelhead, but I can't see any reason smallmouths shouldn't rank right up there with them. (And I grant this same respect to largemouth bass and bluegills, among other fishes.)

Across much of North America the prevailing attitude is different altogether—a fly fisher in Chicago or Minneapolis, for example, is as likely to claim the smallmouth as his or her favorite fish as one of the trout species. Perhaps more likely.

## TELLING SMALLMOUTH FROM LARGEMOUTH

It's easy at first to confuse smallmouth bass with largemouth bass—they do look similar. But they are very different fishes, different habits, different habitats. See page 52 to learn how to tell smallmouth from largemouth bass.

Smallmouth bass.

## TYPES OF SMALLMOUTH RIVERS

In chapter 7 we explored various kinds of rivers, streams, and creeks—so there's no point in doing that again here. If you want to know what a smallmouth bass river is, read my description of a trout river on pages 41 and 42; then remember that smallmouth bass, though they can handle very cold water in winter, need warmish water through a good chunk of the spring, summer, and fall. So rivers flowing through forest, desert, or plains,

from tiny creeks to such massive flows as the West's great Columbia River, may be either trout or smallmouth water depending primarily on just one factor: temperature. Even icy spring creeks and tail-waters can warm sufficiently to provide good smallmouth water well downstream from their sources.

Like trout, smallmouth bass prefer rivers and lakes with rocky beds, though they like water plants, are comfortable in currents from slow to swift, and inhabit water from clear to cloudy.

This forested little river in Pennsylvania gathers itself from several spring creeks upstream. Those chilly spring creeks contain trout, but down this low the water warms too much for trout yet does suit smallmouth bass and, in the big pools (like this one below a millpond), bluegills, crappie, and rock bass.

The Snake River bordering Idaho and Washington is truly *big* smallmouth bass water. It flows through desert canyon, complete with cacti and rattlesnakes.

# TACKLE FOR SMALLMOUTH RIVERS

Here is a list of only that equipment you'll need specifically for smallmouth rivers. You could easily add to this list, but you won't really need to. For other kinds of fishing, you may need some items and not need others listed here. If you have questions or need more detail, refer to chapter 1, "Equipment."

*Fly Line, Rod, Reel:* Use the six-weight outfit described in chapter 1. However, a handy second fly line (which you would logically carry on a second reel-spool) would be a sink-tip line—specifically, a 6-weight with a type-III sinking tip of 10 to 15 feet, typically designated as "WF 6 F/S type III." You can get along fine with just the full-floating line for a long time, but if you fish larger smallmouth rivers, you'll wind up wanting the sink-tip line eventually.

*Leader and Tippet:* Two 7 1/2-foot 1X tapered leaders (three leaders if you get a sink-tip line), one spool of standard 2X tippet.

*Fly Box:* One, capable of containing the larger smallmouth-size flies without crushing them.

*Eyeglasses:* One pair clear and one pair polarized sunglasses (prescription or non-prescription).

*Vest, Pack, or Box:* One vest (or chest or hip pack; forget a tackle box on a stream).

*Gadgets:* One pair of clippers, one pair of forceps, one hook hone.

*Clothing:* See "Clothing" in chapter 1, "Equipment."

*Sunscreen:* Get it, use it.

*Personal:* Water, food, a small flashlight, and toilet paper (a small first-aid kit is always wise).

*Waders:* One pair. Optional only on hot days in midsummer.

*Wading Boots:* Required only if your waders aren't the boot-foot type.

*Wading Staff:* Not required, but I strongly recommend one for safety and ease.

## Flies

Big topic, but I'll do my best to make it small, and simple. The challenge to making fly selection simple, however, is that although various fly shops and online companies carry some of the same flies, they carry different ones too—that's inevitable with the abundance of fly designs out there. So if I give you just a straightforward list, you may not be able to fill it. But the list below includes solid substitute patterns—this gives you plenty of room to round out your collection.

As you continue to fish rivers you will naturally add new flies to your boxes—go ahead; we all do it. Nevertheless, the list that follows will normally provide something your smallmouth will take.

I recommend you get three of each pattern, a total of 15 flies—flies get lost and chewed up and hook-points get broken as a natural result of fishing, so you'll be glad you have extras. For more on flies, see chapter 2, "Flies and the Creatures They Imitate."

## Underwater Flies

1. for imitating small fishes: **Clouser Minnow, Olive Back/White Belly** size 8 (the Clouser rides upside down, so the olive back-hair covers the hook's point, get it?). (Substitutes: Clouser Minnow with any dark back-color and a white belly; Zonker, Olive; Slump Buster, Olive)

2. for general use: **Woolly Bugger, Brown** size 6 with a metal bead or cone for a head. (Substitutes: Woolly Bugger, Olive or Black; Beaded Crystal Bugger, Brown or Olive; Olive Bunny or Rabbit Leech with a metal bead.)

3. for crayfish: **Whitlock's Near Nuff Crayfish, Golden Brown** (or any medium to dark coloring) size 8. (Substitutes: Enrico's Crayfish, Olive; Clouser's Crayfish, Green/Olive; Mercer's Poxyback Crayfish.)

Clouser Minnow     Woolly Bugger

Whitlock's Near Nuff Crayfish     hair bass bug     popper

## Floating Flies

4. for general use: **Hair Bass Bug, Brown** with a *body* (not including the tail) about 1/2-inch long. (Bass-hook sizes are wildly inconsistent, so body length is the best gauge.) If the fly comes with a monofilament-loop snag guard, cut it off. (Substitutes: any hair bass bug with or without rubber legs, eyes, and other variables, in brown, olive, or gray.)
5. for general use: **Cork or Foam Popper in White or Silver or Gray** with a body about 1/2- to 5/8-inch long. (Substitutes: any popper or Sneaky Pete in white or silver or yellow or gray, or frog coloring.)

## WADING

In most smallmouth rivers, you'll do plenty of wading. But I covered wading on pages 44 and 45 so just go there and learn about it. Important: go back and read about wading just *before* you actually wade in a river. It's partly a practical matter, but more important, it's a matter of safety.

## FISHING THE STREAMER

When you fish a streamer fly (such as the Clouser Minnow or the Woolly Bugger), that is designed to imitate a little fish or something like a little fish, you need to get that fly down to the bass, make it swim, and keep it down there as long as possible. Cast a *weighted* streamer—with heavy metal barbell eyes or a metal bead or with a wire core inside its body—out and across-stream or upstream (upstream gives it the most time to sink), and let it drift and sink freely for one or more seconds (more seconds for more depth). When the fly is close to the riverbed and partway downstream, begin retrieving it with short strips of the fly line or, if that makes it rise too far off the bottom, just waggle the rod's tip and do not retrieve. Try to make the fly shimmy and swim down there. You can mend the line if it develops too much belly upstream or downstream and drags the fly too quickly.

Of course you want the fly somewhere down near the bottom, but not down *on* the bottom where it will snag.

Keep the rod's tip down on the water and the rod in line with the fly line—all this helps you *feel* the strike.

---

**LEADER AND TIPPET FOR SMALLMOUTH RIVERS (ALL FLIES)**

**Floating line:** 7 1/2 foot 1X leader, 2 feet 2X tippet
**Sink-tip line:** 7 1/2 foot 1X leader, 2 feet 2X tippet (or no tippet, tie the fly directly onto the point of the leader)

---

With a floating line, a weighted streamer fly can be fished effectively if the water isn't really deep (no deeper normally than, say, four feet). But if the water is deep—and especially if the current is swift—a sink-tip line will really help you get the fly down and keep it down.

## FISHING THE CRAYFISH FLY

Most of the time crayfish crawl among stones, quietly seeking food, but when they're threatened, they dart low and quickly away by pumping their fan-tails. So here's how you fish a crayfish-imitating fly: cast it upstream and let it sink until it touches or almost touches the bottom, and then work it in with quick foot-long strips of the line and brief pauses between strips. The smallmouths are likely to take the fly on the pauses, so when you strip line you'll feel the hook jerk home. Keep the rod's tip down on the water and the rod in line with the fly line, no angles, so you really feel the strike.

In shallower to modestly deep water a floating line is fine, but in the deeper water or larger to big rivers, a sink-tip line may really help keep a crayfish-fly down.

## FISHING THE BASS BUG OR POPPER

In chapter 8 you learned how to fish a popper or hair bug for largemouth bass—well, forget all that. Working a floating fly for smallmouths is different. With smallmouths, toss out the popper or bug, give it a modest twitch right away (just enough to make a fuss but not enough action to scare the fish), let the bug drift quietly (*no* movement) for three or four seconds, then another modest twitch as before, wait three or fours seconds, twitch, and so on.

Try to tug the rod-tip sharply low to the side and then flip it right back to where it started in order to make the bug or popper gurgle—by working the rod-tip this way, you avoid dragging the bug away from the fish. (This is the same technique for working a bug or popper for largemouth bass described on page 55) If the three- to four-second pauses don't work, try only one second up to ten seconds between tugs on the fly—you can even try hard chugs.

Expect to fish a hair bug or popper mostly in slower water, such as back eddies and runs and around boulders and fallen timber that break the current, where the river is two to five feet deep, especially in the morning and evening and on overcast days. But fast water at midday *can* be red hot with a popper...trust me. I've fished smallmouth rivers all over the US, and as productive as streamers and crayfish flies have been for me in those rivers, I've fished hair bugs and poppers almost as often as these subsurface flies—because they keep working (and because fishing them is great fun).

## READING A SMALLMOUTH RIVER

Like a trout river, a smallmouth-bass river holds fish only in certain places. In fact, mostly they're the same places for both fishes. Bass and trout rivers are pretty much the same too. It's tough even for a seasoned fly fisher to tell if a river suits trout or smallmouths just by looking at it, because the main determining factor—water temperature—is invisible. Since both fishes inhabit virtually identical kinds of rivers (even though those rivers can run a broad range), it makes sense they'd find safety and food in the same parts of them. So I'll send you back to chapter 7, "Trout in Rivers" for the lies both trout and smallmouths like, and I'll provide page numbers to make that easy. Then we'll take a look at some holding water you haven't yet seen.

**Riffle, Run** (see page **48**)
**Pool, Bank** (see page **49**)

## Obstruction

By "obstruction," I simply mean anything that breaks the river's flow—an island, a boulder, a fallen tree... Anything large and hard enough to split the current will provide cover for smallmouth; behind and possibly alongside and in front of that obstruction is slowed water where small-mouths may hold.

## Water Plants

There is food—damselfly nymphs, frogs, little fishes, and more—living among aquatic plants in rivers and smallmouth bass know it. So they frequently visit and search through pickerelweed, lilies, water chestnut, and such. Fields of vegetation (like the one behind me in the photo) hold great promise, but even a few sparse plants can surprise you with the number of smallmouths they can attract.

## Eddy

Sometimes a current swings around in a big circle so that along the bank the water is actually moving *up*stream—that whole circle or oval of flow is called an "eddy" or "back eddy," a promising place to seek smallmouths. Eddies normally flow slowly with depth and are some-times productive with a hair bug or popper. They're always worth exploring with a streamer or crayfish fly.

## Other Smallmouth Lies

So we've looked at typical smallmouth water on a river, but there are other smallmouth lies that are many, varied, and hard to define. Just look at it this way: wherever there is some depth, with current running from nonexistent to swift, there may be smallmouths.

Odd pockets next to rapids, seemingly dead backwaters, shadowed rock ledges—these and other features and irregularities in a river may occasionally attract smallmouth bass. Keep an open mind. The bass do.

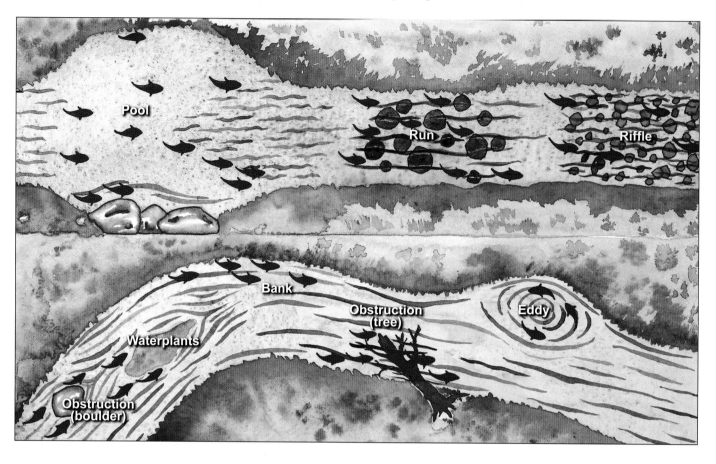

## A DAY ON A SMALLMOUTH RIVER

It's summer. The little river has settled away from its banks of grass and brush leaving but one reminder of the brimming flows of spring: the two, dry bands of gravel that skirt the water and crunch beneath your wading boots. Contentment seems to fill the air. You're glad that working the river is now a comfortable prospect, the river seems to slide cheerfully along, and best of all the bass are happy and eager to satisfy their healthy mid-season appetites. It's about 7:00 a.m.—you came early knowing that the low light of morning and evening tend to offer better smallmouth fishing than glaring midday.

Your eyes scan the river for at least a minute, to see if some clue reveals itself, a crayfish picking through the shallows, a big caddisfly flitting by to reveal a hatch, the rise of a bass in a lazy line of current to suggest a floating fly. You see nothing this obvious. But looking upstream you do notice the way the river rushes into a pool, pauses in the pool's deep center, and breaks swift and shallow to tumble downstream. Your mind tries to picture how you'll fish all that structure. Your fishing partner decides to fish downstream a ways, though not out of sight.

So you strip leader and floating fly line off your reel, work them up the guides of your rod, and then make the safe and logical choice of tying a Clouser Minnow onto your tippet. Before you the river is wide and thin, rippling over cobble. You make some casts, but it's all too shallow to bother with here, so you walk upstream to find an oil-smooth patch of water behind a boulder.

You stay out of the water at first, because the fish could be in close and one step could send them darting in panic. So just back from the clear current, crouching to keep your profile low, you flip the weighted fly upstream, along the near side of the boulder, and let it sink a bit. Then you twitch it lightly, working it slowly enough that it stays down near the riverbed to swim like a baby smallmouth. Within seconds you feel a tug—you tug quickly and firmly back. Now you feel true resistance. You're prepared to give line, but the fish doesn't demand it. You eventually slide an eight-inch smallmouth across the top of the water, hoist him by his little jaw only long enough to back the hook out, and return him quietly to the river.

One cast, one fish. A little fish, granted, but a promising start. Besides, *all* fish feel good when they pull.

You work the Clouser deep through a couple of other pockets without a hit and now stand facing the pool. You crouch low, move up and then toss and work your fly lightly above the shallow lip of the pool, but nothing happens. You work up along the near side of the pool, throwing your fly upstream into the lazy water, stripping it in wherever there is some depth.

It's tempting to work the fly close, so you can see it, but you know that if the smallmouths are close enough for you to see, they'll probably see you too and ignore your fly.

You feel a tug, but then nothing. Could have been a good bass, but it could have been a bluegill or other panfish in the quiet water, whose mouth is just too small to accept the fly. You're tempted to try a smaller fly—panfishes are fun!—but you'd like to give the bass more time while the light is low, so you keep working the Clouser.

The current picks up as you near the head of the pool. Alongside the swirling point of the long, choppy triangle where the water slackens into the quiet belly of the pool, your Clouser simply stops down deep. You tug on the fish and feel his weight. He pulls a deep arc into the rod, thrusts wildly against it. But, after more of this, you press the fish, work him in, and catch his lip to raise him: a pound and a half of golden-olive smallmouth bass comes up. You quickly unhook him. He pauses, bolts for deep water. One perfectly respectable smallmouth caught and released: the day is already a success.

You hook three more bass of about a pound each by working up the long edge of the current tongue and all the water between it and your bank, right up to the rushing head of the pool.

Above the pool, the river divides quietly among odd shapes of sandstone. There are no conventional lies here. Yet there are places for fish. The Clouser might still work, but this looks like crayfish water, so you clip off the Clouser Minnow and tie on a Whitlock's Near Nuff Crayfish. On a slab of gritty rock that seems to melt down into a clear, still backwater you crouch, and move up only to within a few feet of the water's edge—any bass in here will be nervous.

As quietly as possible, with the rod low, you lob the fly to your right, near your bank at the rounded head of the backwater. It lands in the shallows with little commotion. With the rod still low, you scoot the fly in, making it dart, but letting it ride low under its own weight. Then you see a smallmouth swinging in fast from your left. Suddenly you feel the thump as you see the bass flare its wide mouth in the clear water. You tug the hook home and wrestle what turns out to be a stout and perfect two-pound smallmouth—a real prize. You unhook the fish and admire it as it lies quiet in the water for only a moment before darting away.

You work up through all the odd water most anglers would miss—more backwaters, a submerged rock-ledge, a little pool fed by a small channel of lazy flow well off the main river that seemed too small and exposed to hold a decent fish yet did. A couple of fish inhale the fly before your eyes but spit it

out in a flash and you never even feel them. Two others see you and stare back but won't touch the fly. Still, by the time you're through this stretch of odd water you've brought two fine smallmouths and three smaller ones to hand and released them all. Now it's plain hot under a high sun and clear sky.

Another large pool comes next, but the bass are difficult. Most of them turn away from your crayfish fly, and then from the Clouser. Nothing new, smallmouth can be moody. A midday slump. But you switch to a hair bug. Up comes a bass to smack down the chunky little bobbing brown thing in flashes of spray and reflected sunshine. Fishing is good and steady right up to the head of the pool. A floating bug really shouldn't have been the solution to midday sun, but such is fishing...

Finally you hike downstream to find your partner, and you both decide to break for lunch. You drive into town together and you order a salad and a big hamburger that will hold you until dark.

---

You and your friend arrive at a new stretch of the river to find it dappled with the long shadows of late afternoon—the promise of evening is near. But there's plenty of fishing to be done before the sun leaves.

Back to the crayfish fly, which soon hooks a small bass along the edge of a deep run. The boulders out in the body of the flow don't seem right for a crayfish though, and the fly doesn't quite get down where you'd like it. There's always the Clouser Minnow, but you decide a Woolly Bugger with a big metal bead, worked slowly, might be just right. You also decide that your sink-tip line will help the fly penetrate the deep flow, so you switch spools on your reel. Good decisions—working up through the whole run you hook five more smallmouths, land three. Two of them give a satisfying heft when you raise them to back out the fly.

Shadow darkens the river now and only half the disc of the sun shows above the treetops. Good time to try a floating fly. Above the run was a shallow riffle that offered nothing, and now you stand by an eddy alongside a large pool.

You switch back to the floating line and tie on a silvery popper; then you cast it up along the thigh-deep edge of the eddy. You give the fly a twitch, wait, twitch it again, and so on until it's time to pick up the fly. After working the edge water, you throw the popper in front of an exposed boulder ten feet out. The boulder looks so good that you mend the line right away. This will keep the fly out there longer, and makes it jump about right. After your next tug on the line a bass rolls on the popper. You strike, play the fish, and finally release a 1 1/2-pounder.

After you raise and hook three more fish of ten or twelve inches, things slow, yet there's plenty of this long eddy left to fish. You speed up the retrieve of the popper through several casts. Nothing. So you try the opposite—each retrieve is broken by longer pauses until, now well up the eddy, you're letting the fly sit eight seconds between gurgles. That does it. A bass comes lazily to the fly. Then another comes. Finally a last little smallmouth takes the fly as night takes the river.

# CHAPTER 10

# Trout in Lakes

Not nearly everywhere do you get a shot at catching a trout in a lake, at least not in a serious way. For example, I caught a little planted rainbow trout from a pond in the Texas Panhandle one March. I released the fish, but was told it wouldn't last even through spring—a few small hatchery trout struggling to avoid big, predatory largemouth bass, then dying when the water just begins its seasonal warm-up is hardly real trout-lake fishing. (And those bass *were* big—I caught my biggest to date that day.)

In North America, it's mostly the northern states, Canadian provinces, and high country that offer serious trout fishing in lakes. But it's all trade-offs—Idaho and Colorado may offer some fine trout lakes, and Washington and British Columbia may be filled with them, but Virginia is prime smallmouth-bass country and Florida offers largemouth bass practically wherever there is fresh water (even in the big lake surrounded by Walt Disney World!) and a great variety of fascinating saltwater fishes to boot. For every kind of fly fishing you don't get where you live, there's probably another kind you do.

If you do live near trout lakes, you're in for fishing as challenging and rewarding as fishing gets. And as you'll soon see, fishing a trout lake is much more than a few minor tweaks away from fishing the iconic fly fisher's water, the trout river. Personally, I'm a great fan of both trout rivers and trout lakes. The techniques and strategies, the insect hatches and other feed, the patterns of the fish's behavior, and even the tackle are different for trout in lakes than for trout in rivers. I'm glad they are—how dull it would be if fishing a trout lake were really just fishing a big pool in a river. But, not even close.

## LAKES, RESERVOIRS, AND PONDS

Like largemouth bass and bluegills, trout live in natural lakes, reservoirs, and natural and man-made ponds. But I explained all about these waters on page 53 in chapter 8, "Largemouth Bass and Bluegills in Lakes."

### Tackle for Trout Lakes

Here is a list of only the fly equipment you'll need specifically for trout lakes. Sure, there are useful items you could add, but this is a good starting selection and can carry you a long way. For other kinds of fishing, you may need some items not listed here but not need others that are—each of the four chapters on specific types of fishing has its own list. If you have questions about any of these items, refer back to chapter 1, "Equipment."

*Fly Line, Rod, Reel:* Just use the six-weight outfit described in chapter 1, but with one exception: add an extra reel spool loaded with backing and a weight-forward, 6-weight, type III, *full*-sinking fly line, in a dark color (and also eventually a clear "lake line," my favorite, or type II full-sinking line).

*Leader and Tippet:* Two 9-foot 2X and two 12-foot 3X tapered leaders. One spool of 4X and one spool of 3X standard tippet.

*Strike Indicator:* Bring three, preferably big.

*Fly Box:* One, large enough to contain the flies without crushing them.

*Eyeglasses:* One pair of clear glasses and one pair polarized sunglasses (prescription or non).

*Vest, Pack, or Box:* One vest, chest pack, or plastic or rubber tackle box (or tool box). The bags or compartments on a float tube or kick boat may replace a vest or chest pack; in a boat bring a vest or (my preference) a tackle box.

*Gadgets:* One pair of clippers, one pair of forceps, one hook hone.

*Clothing:* See "Clothing" in chapter 1, "Equipment."

*Sunscreen:* Bring it and use it.

*Personal:* Bring water, food, a small first-aid kit, a small flashlight, and toilet paper.

*Waders:* One pair, but only if you'll be fishing from a float tube or kick boat, not a boat.

*Wading Boots:* Useful only if your waders aren't the boot-foot type. Many of the swim fins designed for float tubes and kick boats go on over your bootless feet in stockingfoot waders—no wading boots.

*Swim Fins:* One pair for float tubes or kick boats only.

*Watercraft:* You need one; see chapter 1, "Equipment."

*Life Vest:* Always with a boat, often with an inflatable float tube or kick boat or such (check state law). Safety...

*Anchors:* Two for a boat, one for a float tube or kick boat. Eight-pound anchors for all (except boats over twelve feet). Thirty five feet of 1/2-inch rope for each anchor.

### Flies

A simple list of popular fly patterns for your trout-lake fishing would make things neat and easy...but it might fail—fly shops and catalogs can carry only so many flies in so many sizes, consequently you might hunt all over and still wind up with that list unfilled. That's why I'll give you a list with *substitutes*. If, for example, you can't find the Chan's Chironomid Pupa, black/red in size 14, you can almost certainly find one of its three substitute Chironomid patterns.

As you continue to fish trout lakes you will add new fly patterns to your boxes—a fly that a friend or a fly shop recommends or that you see in a magazine… Nevertheless, the list that follows will normally provide something similar to the insect that's hatching or the creature the trout are eating or just something that'll work.

I recommend you get three of each pattern and size, 30 flies in all—you're going to break off and lose flies as a natural part of fishing them, so you'll be glad you have back-ups. (For more on flies, see chapter 2, "Flies and the Creatures They Imitate.")

## Nymphs and a Streamer   *caddis Flyshop has my river Fly order*

1. for Chironomid pupae: **Chan's Chironomid Pupa, Black/Red** size 14, 12. (Substitutes: Sno Cone [Ice Cream Cone], Maroon; Jumbo Juju Chironomid, Blood Red; Stalcup Chironomid, Black.)
2. for mayfly nymphs: **Gold Ribbed Hare's Ear** size 14. (Substitutes: Anatomical *Callibaetis,* Feather Duster, Pheasant Tail Nymph.)
3. for damselfly nymphs: Imitations come and go, so take whatever fly pattern is available, unweighted (no metal bead for a head or lead-wire inside the body) size 10 (if the fly's abdomen extends off the hook, get size 12).
4. for dragonfly nymphs: **Sparkle Furry Dragon** size 6. (Substitutes: Carey Special; Woolly Bugger, Olive [tear the tail off short]; Kaufmann's Lake Dragon.)
5. for scuds: **Scud, Olive** size 12. (Substitutes: Bead Head Scud, Olive; Stalcup Softex Scud, Olive; Baggie Shrimp, Olive.)
6. for leeches: **Woolly Bugger, Black** size 8. (Substitutes: Janssen Marabou Leech, Black; Seal Bugger, Black; Halebopp Leech, Black.)
7. for water boatmen and back swimmers: **Morris Boatman** (Skip's Boatman) size 14. (Substitutes: Zug Bug; Gold Ribbed Hare's Ear, Black [or brown]; any current waterboatman imitation your fly shop or mail-order house recommends.)

## Emergers and Dry Flies

8. for mayflies: **Morris Emerger,** *Callibaetis* size 14. (Substitutes: Parachute Adams; Sparkle Dun, Olive; Adams [standard].)
9. for caddisflies: **Elk Hair Caddis** (the original, with a tan body) size 12. (Substitutes: Goddard Caddis, Parachute Caddis [original, with a tan body], Hemingway Caddis.)

If you cannot find one or more of these fly patterns at your local fly shop or online, ask a salesman to recommend something comparable.

## TROUT-LAKE FEED

The most important hatching insect on trout lakes is the Chironomid—you'll see it often, squirming to the water's surface, wriggling there from its shuck, popping out to look like a mosquito, and then flying off. After the Chironomid in importance are a medium-size mayfly called *"Callibaetis,"* the substantial but slender damselfly that shimmies towards shore not far under the water's surface to finally climb out and hatch, and a variety of caddisflies. All these insects

*Callibaetis* dun

Chan's Chironomid Pupa | Gold Ribbed Hare's Ear | Green Damsel | Sparkle Furry Dragon

Scud | Woolly Bugger | Morris Boatman | Morris Emerger | Elk Hair Caddis expose themselves to trout when they hatch. Other important trout-feed in lakes includes the hulking dragonfly nymph, the disgusting and slimy leech, and the little shrimplike scud.

For more details on these creatures, see chapter 2, "Flies and the Creatures They Imitate."

## TROLLING WITH A SINKING LINE

Trolling is a very effective way to fish a lake, and it's really a boon on an unfamiliar lake because you can fish while exploring. The fly swims close down along the lake's bed—where trout spend most of their time—and stays there as the angler tows it through lots of promising water, seeing lots of the lake in the process.

To troll, rig up your type III full-sinking line with a 9-foot 2X tapered leader and two feet of 3X tippet. Tie on a size 14 Gold Ribbed Hare's Ear (or one of its substitutes) or, if you know the trout are large (at least 14 inches long on average), a size-6 Sparkle Furry Dragon (or one of its substitutes). Use the mono loop knot to tie on the fly.

Make a long cast behind your boat or float tube. If you're in a boat, set the rod down well inside so it *stays* inside when a big trout hits. Begin rowing or kicking away from the line, trying to hold to water around 12 to 20 feet deep. Strip a few feet of fly line off the reel, row or kick away, pull off another few feet, row or kick...until half to nearly all of your line is out, only about a dozen feet of line remaining on the reel. Don't just strip out lots of line and then start moving because the fly will end up on the bottom of the lake, snagged. A strike can come at any time, and when it does, raise the rod-tip to set the hook.

**TROLLING**

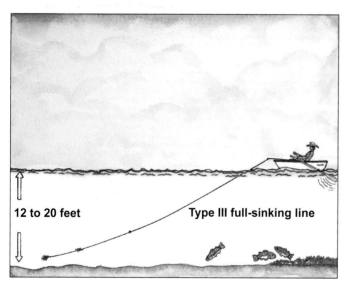

12 to 20 feet          Type III full-sinking line

Keep trolling by rowing or finning *slowly* along. You can raise the rod tip and drop it now and then to put some natural variation into the fly's swimming. You want the fly to stay down near the lake's bed, so expect to snag a plant or bit of bark now and then and to occasionally lose a fly.

Sometimes you won't know that your fly is dragging a scrap of water plant, a leaf or twig—so pull in all the line about

every ten minutes and pile it carefully on the bottom of the boat or, in a float tube or kick boat, on your stripping apron so the line won't tangle, and check the fly. Bring the fly to hand and make sure nothing clings to any part of the fly; then clean off the fly if necessary. A trout normally won't take a fly that's dragging even a shred of weed or such. When the fly is ready, cast it out and follow the same process as before to work out the line. (With the line already out of the rod, you can clamp the line between your knees as you row a boat, pulling out a few feet at a time.)

## THE COUNTDOWN METHOD

Trolling is one way to fish a sinking line in a trout lake, casting a sinking line is the other. To cast a sinking line, first you anchor (remember: two anchors for a boat but just one for a float tube or kick boat), and then employ the countdown method. This method is best when the trout are concentrated, typically over a shoal (which we'll explore soon).

Rig up your type III full-sinking line (though eventually it could be a type I or type II or a clear lake line) with a 9-foot 2X tapered leader and two feet of 3X tippet. Use the mono loop knot. Start with either of the flies recommended for trolling.

Here's how you perform the countdown method:

1. Make a long cast; then begin counting (I say "one-one-thousand, two-one-thousand, three-one-thousand...) until you think the fly is down at the right depth. Let's suppose you counted to twelve this time. (*Do not* subconsciously draw in the line as you count—not an inch.)

2. Using the hand-twist retrieve (see page 36), work the line and fly in. If you feel no resistance, and the fly comes up clean, then add to the count by one; in this case, that's now thirteen.

3. If there's still no snagging, add one more to the count. Keep casting and adding to your count each time. When you feel a snag or find a bit of green water plant or such on the fly, you've got your number. Back off your count by one—so if you finally caught the bottom at 16, fish the fly at a count of 15.

If you'd snagged the first time you counted (which we decided was to 12), you'd next count to 11, and then keep backing off by one count with each cast until the fly didn't snag—then you'd have your depth.

**THE COUNTDOWN METHOD**

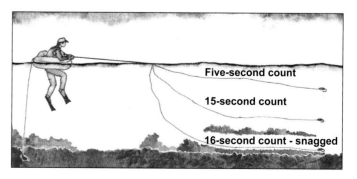

Five-second count

15-second count

16-second count - snagged

Whenever you retrieve a sinking line in a lake, keep the rod-tip down on the water and the rod in line with the fly line. Avoid *consistently* that hanging curve of slack that forms when the rod-tip is raised—it kills all your sensitivity to a take of the fly.

## FISHING THE SURFACE

Fishing a dry fly or emerger-fly on the surface of the water or a nymph just below the surface with a floating line are actually the easiest ways to fish a trout lake—casting is the most relaxed with the light line that almost hovers, and whatever's going on with the fly is up in plain sight.

Most of the time on most trout lakes, a deep nymph (or streamer) is the most productive way to fish. But sometimes a fly on or in or just under the surface is best, and it can be great fun!

Rig a 9-foot 2X tapered leader and two and a half feet of 4X tippet with your floating line and a dry fly, emerger, or nymph (which fly? try an Elk Hair Caddis) if you see trout up feeding at the water's surface. They'll be making those ringed wavelets we call rises, or violently slamming something down.

When you see plenty of surface activity (just a few rising trout aren't enough), cast your fly to land within two feet or so of the trout, or just toss your fly out among a bunch of working fish. Twitch (no more than a twitch) and pause a dry fly or emerger. Swim a nymph slowly enough to keep it submerged a few inches, using the hand-twist retrieve. Set the hook when the trout makes a splash or swirl at the floating fly or, with a submerged nymph, when you just feel the resistance down the line—which is why you keep the rod-tip down on the water and the rod pointed straight down the line—to eliminate all slack so you can immediately feel the fish take your nymph.

**CASTING TO RISING TROUT**

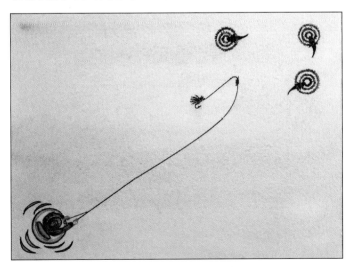

## CHIRONOMID FISHING

Over the past three decades or so, "Chironomid fishing," suspending a Chironomid-pupa fly over a lake-bed, has become a huge component of lake fishing for trout. The fly stays down with the trout much longer than most fishing methods allow and seems to wriggle like a real Chironomid pupa. Here's how it's done:

1. Find a shoal (I'll explain shoals soon).
2. Look closely for the signs of a Chironomid hatch: wormlike pupae wriggling at the water's surface to hatch; adults popping out onto the surface to look like mosquitoes; glassy, white-bearded abandoned shucks awash *in* the lake's surface.
3. Anchor your boat or float tube (two anchors for a boat, one for a float tube) amid the hatch, typically in water about eight to 16 feet deep (though Chironomid fishing can work in water shallower and deeper than this range).
4. Rig up a 12-foot 3X tapered leader with four feet of 4X tippet, and tie a weighted Chironomid-pupa fly matching the size of the natural onto the tippet (the Chan's Chironomid Pupa or one of its substitutes) using the mono loop knot.
5. Check the depth by clamping forceps firmly onto the bend of the fly (not the body) and lowering the fly and forceps slowly down. Once they touch the bottom, raise them and set the strike indicator on the leader just one foot short of the depth (so if the depth is 13 feet, the indicator should be 12 feet up the tippet and leader from the fly). Remove the forceps.
6. Cast the rig well out across the wind (if there is a light wind), and then do nothing but watch the indicator until the wind has carried the line straight downwind.
7. When the line and indicator *are* straight downwind, work them back in slow, three-inch draws of line between pauses of about 12 seconds. (If there's no wind, cast out the rig, wait 60 seconds, and then draw in the fly with the same retrieve I just described.)
8. Set the hook immediately if the indicator dips or twitches or charges away—it may do any one of these.

Chironomid fishing is usually best if you see Chironomids hatching from a shoal. But Chironomid fishing can be good any time, because it's a very natural and convincing technique and the trout regularly see and eat the pupae.

**CHIRONOMID FISHING**

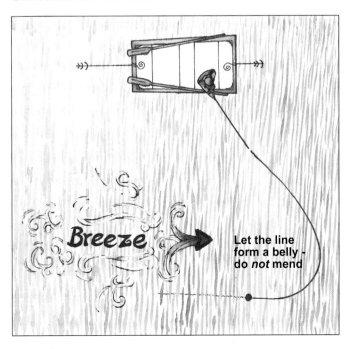

Breeze

Let the line form a belly - do *not* mend

# READING A TROUT LAKE

As a rule, a few areas of a lake tend to attract trout the most consistently and in the highest concentrations, while many other areas of a lake will hold trout only rarely, (though it's always wise to keep an open mind—fishing rules can be dead wrong). Described below are the most reliable places to find trout in lakes.

In a very clear lake you can see some submerged features (shoals, springs...). The limited clarity of many lakes will require you to find underwater features with a topographical map of the lake (sometimes included in fishing guidebooks), by judging the shoreline (it probably continues down into the water at the same angle it enters it), by trolling and noting depth (which allows you to fish while you explore), by dropping your anchor here or there for a mental picture of the lake bed's structure (the slowest method), or by all these methods.

You can also watch other anglers—if they know the lake, they'll head for the best areas. The ideal tool for seeing what's down in a lake is the fish-finder, a sonar device. But fish-finders are expensive, so I suggest you wait to decide whether trout-lake fishing is for you before shopping for one. Don't fret—the information that follows will help you find trout in a lake without a fish finder.

## Shoal

A shoal is a relatively broad, flat section of a lake's bed that deepens gradually from the shoreline out. Because a shoal is fairly shallow and gets a heavy daily dose of nourishing sunlight, it grows an abundant crop of trout-foods: mayfly nymphs, Chironomids, leeches, the works. Trout know this, and visit shoals frequently.

Often, you'll find a shoal in a bay, but some shoals extend out from a straight shoreline. In a clear lake, a shoal will appear as pale or, if weedy, green area.

Shoals are generally your most promising shot at finding trout in a lake.

## Drop-Off

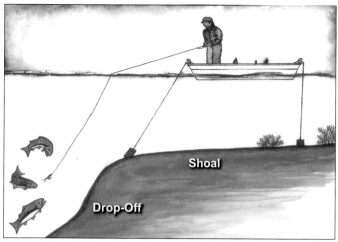

Typically, the outer rim of a shoal turns downward into the depths; this rim is called a "drop-off." In clear water you'll see it as dark water meeting the lighter shoal. When trout aren't up on a shoal, they're often cruising the edge of the drop-off or just below it.

## Feeder Stream

Where a creek or river enters a lake, trout may gather any time, but especially will when the lake is uncomfortably warm—that cold oxygen-rich flow provides real relief.

## Springs

For the same reasons feeder streams attract trout in lakes—specifically, oxygen and cooler water—springs attract trout. Springs, if you can see them, appear as pale patches on the bottom, and tend to be found in groups.

## Bay

A notch in the shoreline of a lake is called a "bay." A bay may cover a quarter of the lake or span only twice the length of your boat. Actually, any irregularity along a lake's shoreline can attract trout. A bay often lies between points of land (trout will sometimes hang around points) with a bed that is a shoal, so altogether there can be lots of good structure—trout may hold along the shoreline, down on the shoal, or feed at the surface right out in the bay's center.

## Shallows

In spring and fall, you may find trout feeding in the cold and oxygen-rich shallows. They'll hold there near fallen trees, overhanging limbs and brush, all around beds of water-plants, and other cover. Or they'll just pick their way along the shoreline seeking feed—and there is typically plenty of that in shallow water. Approach shallow trout with care—long quiet casts, long leaders and tippets—they are easily spooked.

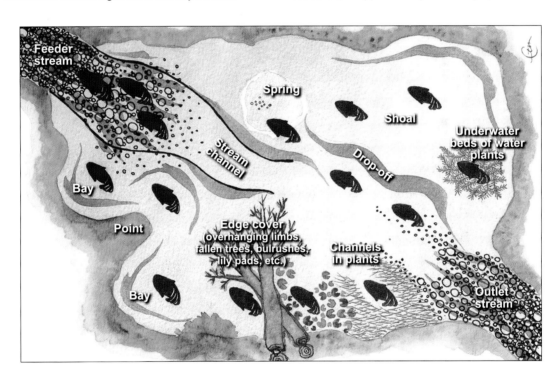

---

## A DAY ON A TROUT LAKE

It's early May, and the brisk air seems to resist warming under the morning sunshine. Only a line of little cottony clouds breaks up the vast blue above. The lake lies before you, an oval of calm a deeper blue than the sky. You snoop around the cobble and waterlogged wood in the lake's edge. You find good things there. A scud paddles aimlessly over silt. A blackish leech undulates away when you raise a shallow stone.

Soon you're rigged and rowing in your pram away from the boat launch. You watch your friend on shore setting up his pontoon boat. He waves. Though you may not talk with him again until you meet at the boat launch when it's all over, you'll stay within sight of one another on the little lake. Now though, how to start out...

Trolling makes sense on this unfamiliar water, but first, you want to find out if the slope of that shoreline off to your left continues into the lake as a shoal—a lake shoal is always worth investigating. You arrive there, and then press on the oars to halt your boat. You take a hard look around. An easy breeze crinkles the water in patches. Swallows swarm and swoop over the placid water around you, skimming and briefly pocking the surface. Feeding? On what? You look closer. The water is blank, at first. Then a twitching tiny worm wriggles up through the surface of the water, looks for a moment like an upright stick, pops from its shuck to match a mosquito. It buzzes away, leaving a sort of hollow, glassy tube with a miniscule white beard—the discarded shuck of the hatched Chironomid.

More gleaming shucks appear as you near the swooping birds. But there are no rises, just the riselike ringed wavelets left by the occasional touch of a swallow. The trout, of course, are almost certainly taking advantage of the hatch, just not at the surface. So you glide on into the center of the emerging Chironomids (you see one squeezing free of its shuck or standing on the water every foot or two now), and set your anchors. Onto the short, level section of leader nail-knotted to your floating line you tie a 12-foot tapered leader with a 3X point, and then tie four feet of 4X tippet to that point. You set a strike indicator temporarily up the leader. A shuck from the water's surface lies alongside a size-14 Chan's Chironomid Pupa in a puddle in your palm, both close in size. So you tie on the fly to swing freely from a mono loop knot. By clamping your forceps on the bend of the hook and lowering them, you set the strike indicator up the tapered leader one foot short of the water's depth.

You're ready.

A smooth, patient, open cast—the best insurance against a mid-air tangle—carries fly and indicator out. You wait a full minute to let the fly descend. Now it's all about that strike indicator. You stare, and stare... The indicator sits quietly on the calm water between your little pulls on it. Fifteen minutes later, nothing has bothered the indicator, so you move to another part of the shoal a couple of hundred feet away.

Anchors set, indicator set, a cast completed, and a few minutes later the indicator dives. You pull, and up and out comes a somersaulting rainbow trout.

A breeze rises and wavelets bounce the indicator contentedly through the next two passes. On the third cast, it seems only to stall—and you instantly remind yourself that *anything* the indicator does that's even slightly suspicious deserves a hook-set. Out somersaults another trout.

Fishing is good for another two hours. Then the hatch slows, and soon, so does the Chironomid fishing. Time to eat lunch and consider your next move. No rush.

After eating and just relaxing a while, you survey the lake, but see no rises, no swooping birds over the water, no other anglers playing fish. So you decide to troll. You rig up your full-sinking type III line and a 9-foot 2X tapered leader with two feet of 3X tippet and a Sparkle Furry Dragon on a mono loop knot. You cast it all well out, set the reel over the boat seat, and start slowly rowing. Occasionally you feed out a few feet of line. Finally, almost all the line is out. You follow the shoreline, trying to manage your depth. Ten minutes later the rod-tip bounces. You grab the rod and put tension on the fish. It leaps—about three pounds of angry rainbow trout.

Over the next hour the rod-tip jumps five more times; you land another rainbow and two brown trout running 13 to 17 inches. This is simply good, steady fishing, until it dies. So you stop, and take another long look around.

Nothing to your left, or straight ahead, but to your right... the softly expanding circles of a trout's rise stand in plain relief against the calm surface. Another rise appears a dozen feet away from the first, then two more.

Soon you're rowing quietly towards the rises. As you near them you slow way down, approaching with real stealth. A close look reveals flying ants scattered across the water. You pluck one up and see that it's brown, nearly matching a size-14 hook. The closest dry fly you have is an Elk Hair Caddis, though it's a bit large and will stand much higher than the half-drowned ants. You trim off the fibers along the underside of the fly's body with your clippers. Now the fly will press its bulk down on the water. The body is light, but tannish-brown isn't so far from brown. The wing is far too pale, but they won't get much of a look at a wing that's up in the air—besides, you know that ants crash to the water in messy heaps, and won't all look the same from below, so your sheared fly is worth a shot. You tie it onto two and a half feet of 4X tippet that's tied to a 9-foot 2X tapered leader with a full-floating line, and work a little floatant into the fly and along the tippet and leader.

Your boat is now a comfortable cast from the nearest risers. You throw the fly out there among them. You give the fly only the faintest twitch now and then, to make it behave like the struggling ants (and to obscure the fly's inaccuracies). Eventually, a trout drops his nose over it, and you set the hook. He thrashes on top for a moment, then runs hard straight away from you. You let the fish tire himself by letting him strip line off the reel. When he halts, you press him and warily reel in loose line—then snap your hand away from the reel handle as he once again charges away. Eventually, a two-and-a-half-pound rainbow lies in your net. You unhook him with care and hold him lightly underwater until he thrusts from the cradle of your hands.

You flick the sodden fly with a lively stroke to snap it dry. You keep putting it out there, giving it a little action, and hook another trout, and pretty soon, another.

An hour and a half later the ants are all but gone as the rises grow fewer and fewer. But you hooked half a dozen trout and landed four. Great fun!

It's not over yet, though. Clouds drifted overhead during the action with the ants to stall the rising heat and inspire substantial *Callibaetis* mayflies to pop from their shucks onto the water and display their mottled wings. The trout are all for it and continue their random rises as you switch to a Morris Emerger, *Callibaetis* and do just what you were doing with the ants, except now you're looking for fish over shallower water, around eight to 20 feet deep, over shoals with weeds. This adds another wonderful couple of hours to your surface fishing. Until it dies as the clouds drift away.

The clear sky reveals the sun just beginning to settle atop the tree line, half the lake in shade. In that shade you see something else.

What you see is a rise, and soon, another a few feet away from it. Then another, all in a row—clearly this is one fish working the surface in a pattern, "path rising." You row out as the trout rises again. You resist the oars to halt quietly a modest cast from the next rise. The Morris Emerger, *Callibaetis* on your tippet doesn't quite match the *Callibaetis* spinners you're seeing on the lake's surface, but it's not far off either. You put the fly right where the next rise ought to show. The flat water wrinkles around your fly, you tug, a trout sails up in panic. It's going to be a fine evening.

# CHAPTER 11

# Fine Points that Matter

The finer points of fly fishing that we'll examine here really do count—a solid grasp of the first six will definitely catch you more fish, and understanding the seventh point will bring you into harmony with your fellow fly-fishers (much more satisfying than leaving scowls on the faces of the anglers you encounter). The eighth point I'll leave you to ponder.

## OBSERVATION

I honestly believe that only in rare situations can an angler consistently catch fish without being observant. To say that so-and-so is a good fly fisher for someone who isn't observant is like saying some guy is pretty wealthy considering that he's flat broke. That's how important it is to pay attention. It's always wise to just stop and look around when you first arrive at the water, before you wet a fly. Equally wise to keep stopping and looking periodically throughout the day.

Look out over the water, any water—a fish may show, a mist of insects may hover, the far side of a creek may darken to suggest depth in a way that is much more promising than a glance would reveal. Look down, around your feet—stonefly shucks may cling to rocks, scuds may putter about the shallows, a mayfly spinner may lie awash on the water as its lifeless splayed wings shift with the swells. All sorts of clues may reveal themselves to the watchful eye: bluegills hovering over the pale disks of their nests, a crayfish picking at something on a mossy rock. Look far, look near, on the water, under the water, anywhere even near the water. Look at the shoreline, at the slope of the land above the lake or river. Look at other fishermen to see what they're doing and if it's working. Look at everything. If you do, you'll see or just sense clues that will help you fish effectively, regardless of experience. It's a given.

## STEALTH

How you approach a fish, be it a bluegill, bass, or trout, plays a critical role in whether or not you catch that fish. Remember the rule I'm about to tell you, whatever that takes—repeat it four times after every meal (and snack); write it backwards in nontoxic ink across your forehead and look frequently into a mirror; learn Russian and then pay a Russian to follow you around and bark it at you the whole time you're fishing—whatever it takes. Okay, here's The Rule: *If a fish knows you're there, or senses danger of any sort, it will flee, or at least will ignore your fly.* Why would a terrified fish even *think* about eating? I mean, if a Bengal tiger were about to sink its fangs into your leg, would your response be to reach for a sandwich?

The obvious mistake is to let the fish see you. If you're fishing a river, stay out of sight by casting *up*stream (typically, up and out, at an angle, so the leader doesn't land over of the fish). Fish (trout, smallmouth bass...) must face into the current, so they see mainly to their sides and upstream, not downstream. If the water is clear, low, or slow-moving, and the fish are shallow or holding up close to the surface—and especially if two or more of these factors are in play—you may not only need to approach from downstream but to do it crouching low and staying back from the water.

You can't always approach river fish from downstream, so at times a downstream cast of a dry fly or nymph is best. Sometimes you really shouldn't fish upstream, as when streamer fishing for trout.

You can spook fish in other ways than being seen: slapping down the fly, the line, or both; dropping the fly too near the fish, casting the line too near the fish; passing your shadow (or your rod's shadow) over or near the fish; wading noisily; thumping the bottom of a boat or making a ruckus in a

At lake, river, or bay, the observant fly fisher—the one who seems to notice everything—tends to get the best fishing and, consequently, have the most fun

Stealth—a low approach and staying well downstream from the fish—hooked me the skittish brown trout that took my grasshopper fly along the shady bank.

boat or float tube; coming too near the fish in a boat or float tube...the list goes on, but you get the idea.

A moving shadow means danger to fish.

There are variables. If the water is colored, the fish won't be as easily spooked as in clear water. If the fish are feeding deep, they'll be less flighty than fish feeding in shallow water or near the surface. If the water is swift and broken, the fish will have lots of distractions and obstacles to keep them from noticing or even seeing you. All that aside, never disregard stealth.

## JUST THE BASICS

**The elements of The Rule about stealth:**

1. Keep The Rule always in mind as you fish.
2. Do not let the fish see you—some distance helps.
3. Cast upstream (and perhaps crouch low) on a river (normally).
4. Never let your shadow pass over or near fish.
5. Avoid making sounds in the water; bumping the bottom of a boat or wading roughly are typical ways.
6. Clear and shallow water, fish holding near the surface, slow currents, or standing water require more stealth than colored water, deep fish, or broken currents.

## PRESENTATION

To fly-fishers, the term "presentation" refers to how a fly is delivered and worked—how it's "presented" to a fish. Is the fly splatted down or set lightly upon the water? Does it float freely in the current or does it drag or twitch or skim across it? Does it bounce along the cobble at the bottom of a riffle or ride up closer to the water's surface?

Part of presentation is about The Rule about stealth (which we just examined), specifically, the part about getting the fly in front of the fish without frightening him. A bad presentation that would scare a fish would be to splat the fly down on the fish's nose or drop the line over the fish or too near it. But there are exceptions. For example, a grasshopper fly smacked down by a trout seeking grasshoppers could be just right.

So delivering the fly in a way that doesn't alarm the fish is part of effective presentation. Another part is how the fly behaves.

The fly must behave in a way that convinces the fish rather than arousing his suspicions. Let's say mayflies are hatching in a river, sedately riding atop the currents. This means your fly must do the same—ride the currents quietly with no unnatural draw from the leader. Perhaps, though, caddis adults are skimming the water—then a drag-free fly is totally out of place. So you twitch your fly, make it skid across the water now and then. A streamer fly that imitates a baby smallmouth bass?—it'd better swim pretty much the way a baby smallmouth swims.

So, presentation is mainly about casting, line handing, and strategy. But it's also about how you rig up. Too little distance between your Bitch Creek nymph and the strike indicator means the fly can't drop down to the bed of the river. Too thick a tippet will be too stiff to allow your size-20 Griffith's Gnat to drift naturally with the current. You get the idea.

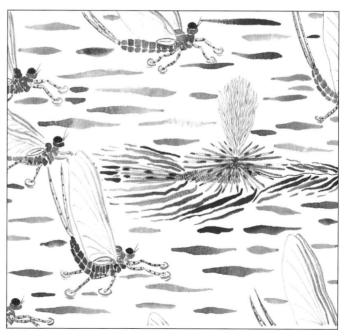
No mistaking this Parachute Adams for another mayfly dun—it's dragging across the current while the duns drift naturally.

# SELECTIVITY

There are times when smallmouth bass, largemouth bass, and even bluegills and the common carp—along with some saltwater species—are as reluctant to take flies as any trout. That reluctance may be due to fear, a full belly, or plain moodiness, but when fish are concentrating on a specific insect, tiny fish, or other food type and ignoring all else, we call this behavior "selectivity." Of all the species fly-fishers seek, trout are the most frequently selective. With trout, selectivity normally accompanies a hatch of insects; for example, olive-bodied mayflies emerge in steady abundance on the current of an October river. The trout try a few, like the taste and now consider them safe eating, and suddenly any fly that doesn't look and act like a mayfly dun drifts past the feeding fish untouched.

So just how precisely must that fly match those hatching mayflies for those trout to take it? That really depends on the particular trout and the particular water they inhabit. If they're hard-fished brown trout (the naturally wariest of trout) in a rich, clear spring creek, you'd better present a fly of proper size and form (a Parachute Adams, perhaps?), on fine tippet, with a long and convincingly natural drift, right down the feeding line of a fish. If, on the other hand, they're hungry cutthroat trout (generally slow learners) rising on a stream where insects are sparse and anglers are rare, you can probably get away with an oversize fly of questionable form roughly fished. Still, even backwoods trout can have their moods...

As I mentioned, selectivity *can* occur with other species than trout—I've seen largemouth bass selective to adult dragonflies, smallmouth bass to pale mayfly duns, and bluegills to damselfly adults. Most of the many and varied fishes fly-fishers seek can turn selective under the right circumstances. Keep selectivity in the back of your mind whenever you fish.

It there's a hatch, fly size should be close to insect size.

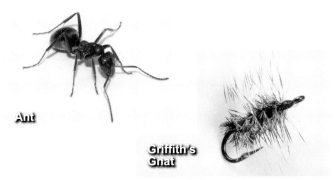

Ant

Griffith's Gnat

Even when you someday carry several boxes stuffed with flies of many sizes, shapes, and colors, you'll still get stuck without *just* the right pattern on occasion. But you can often make do with what you have.

Here is a tiny ant next to a Griffith's Gnat. The Gnat was designed to imitate a hatching midge. Fortunately, trout don't know what flies are *supposed* to represent. Trout see an ant as a black body with legs. The Griffith's Gnat has a dark body and feather fibers for legs, so if it matches the size of the ant and is made to drift like yet another ant, even some picky trout may overlook the differences.

## JUST THE BASICS

### Understanding and dealing with selectivity:

1. "Selectivity" occurs when fish concentrate their feeding on one specific creature.
2. Selectivity occurs most commonly with trout.
3. Fish a fly that matches the creature on which the fish are focused, and make your fly act like that creature.
4. The pickiness of selective fish varies.
5. Keep selectivity in the back of your mind when fishing.

## EXPERIMENTATION, OPEN MIND

To me, experimentation in fly fishing is varying the retrieve of a Clouser Minnow or cutting off the Parachute Adams that's been reliably hooking rainbows during a mayfly hatch and tying on a Brooks' Sprout, *Callibaetis* of the same size simply to see if the fish take an emerger better than a dry fly. Simply put: testing alternatives and theories.

Open-minded fishing from my perspective is a few solid clicks past experimentation—it leans towards somewhat crazy stuff: drifting an unnatural and oversize Royal Wulff or Chernobyl Ant through trout clearly feeding on adult caddisflies, following some trickle that meanders way off the main river and seems far too small to hold smallmouth bass just to see what you find, throwing your nymph into edge water that seems too shallow and too swift to hold a trout. Odd and even illogical tactics like these—sometimes the dead opposite of conventional practice—can turn lousy fishing into fishing that's fast.

Experimentation is always worthwhile because it may improve your fishing and usually adds to your understanding of our sport. The crazy stuff is different, normally the result of crazy fish behavior—desperate measures for when all else fails. Of course, the strategies I've been teaching you throughout this book and the videos are sound, and should provide the foundation of your fishing. But if conventional fails, try unconventional.

In the small and gentle spring creek in the background where tiny dry and emerger-flies like the Morris Emerger on the right are the norm, a big Bitch Creek nymph like the one on the left is a wild choice—but it may be a good one. Start out with a conventional approach. But when all the standard options fail, never hesitate to try a fly or retrieve or technique that under the circumstances seems unlikely or even ridiculous.

## PATIENCE AND PERSERVERANCE

Take up anything new and it'll feel foreign, clumsy, and confusing at first. I've done my best to make fly fishing as little of these things for you as I can. But I'm no magician—I can't make a seasoned fly fisher out of you in days or weeks or even months. So you're going to have to stick with this as your skills and knowledge grow and your instincts kick in. You're at a wonderful point in this journey, though, where everything is new—your first trout, your first trout on a nymph, your first smallmouth bass, your first perfectly timed cast that makes the line seem to sail miraculously out by its own will, and a hundred other glorious firsts. Don't waste these—savor them all.

Not all firsts are glorious, though—your first fishless day, your first tangled leader, your first fly snagged on a back cast in the high limbs of a tree... These and other misfortunes will always be part of your fishing; at first, though, they'll be a particularly common part. If you expect to work a rising trout like a pro on your first fishing trip, if you can't stand to see someone cast better or further or catch more fish than you, this grand sport will bring you only frustration. So be patient, accept that you'll grow as a fly fisher over time and that there's no other way to grow, and be humble. But if you don't learn humility on your own, that's alright, the fish will teach it to you.

## COURTESY

The best rule about courtesy on fishing water is the Golden Rule of all behavior, it's biblical: So in everything, do to others what you would have them do to you. If you were fishing a riffle and someone waded up right in front of you, would you start tallying in your head what it would cost to put out a hit on this guy? Simply put: if you don't get in other anglers' way and don't disturb their fishing or their solitude, you'll get along with them. Here are a few general guidelines:

1. Keep your distance. For example, if you come to a long stretch of river and find an angler fishing there, move down at least a run, riffle, or pool away before fishing. It would be rude to cut in nearby upstream. If there are lots of anglers, however, just try to keep as much space between you and the nearest angler as reasonably possible—the distance rule is flexible, based largely on angler density.

2. When passing other anglers along a river or shoreline, try to stay well back from them and be quiet. If you must come fairly close to pass at all, politely tell them you're coming through so you don't get hit with a back cast.

3. Keep conversation low and spare when others are fishing nearby—it's shocking how efficiently sound travels over water, and nobody (other than perhaps your fishing partner...or not) wants to hear you complain about your boss or ramble on about your gallbladder surgery while they fish.

4. If you're coming into an area on a lake where others are already fishing, slow your outboard motor and putter quietly partway in; then row the last bit going lightly on the oars. If you're rowing the whole way, again, come in quietly. Other anglers will appreciate the courtesy, and you won't alarm the fish you came to catch.

5. Respect private property and follow the local access laws (which vary from state to state, from province to Canadian province).

6. If you'd prefer that fisherman down from you were casting a fly rod rather than a spinning rod and releasing fish rather than killing them, well...there's not much you can do about it. Any angler who follows the law and shows common courtesy towards other anglers has every right to do as they wish. Respect those rights—and never act like a fly-fishing snob.

7. No one likes being stared at, so don't stare at other anglers. But noting what other anglers are doing can improve your fishing—especially if they're catching fish—so watch, but casually, from a distance.

## CATCH-AND-RELEASE

It's often difficult for the average person to understand why anyone would hook and land a fish, and then return it alive to the water—the point of fishing is to bring fish home for the table, right? Well, long ago, sure. But things have changed. Now, ever more anglers share about the same amount of fishing water as there was a hundred years ago, when, for example, the population of the United States was less than a third of what it is today.

Too many anglers all bent on bringing home dinner can threaten to wipe out native fish that over millennia have evolved to perfectly suit a particular lake or river. You can fill fish-depleted water with hatchery-raised substitutes—but that's expensive, and these pampered, naïve, sometimes unhealthy factory-fish can fail to satisfy an experienced angler who wants a little challenge and a natural fishing experience. There are some wise hatchery programs, and they provide a lot of fine sport in waters where fish can thrive but cannot spawn, so hatcheries do have their place. But is their purpose to replace the ancient, wild strains of trout, salmon, and other fishes we've destroyed in our insistence on killing what we catch? Most fly-fishers, and many other anglers, say No.

The alternative to extensive hatchery programs is "catch-and-release," hooking fish on barbless hooks, handling those fish with care, and turning them back to their waters unharmed. You've got to make your own mind up on this one—I'm a teacher, not an ethical or spiritual advisor. But I can tell you this much: seeing an elegantly spotted trout or thick, muscular bass at my feet, watching it accept its freedom from the hook and show its recovery in the testing of its fins until, finally, it thrusts away whole...to me, that's just grand.

# CHAPTER 12

# Other Fishes

The trout, largemouth bass, smallmouth bass, and bluegill we explored in chapters 7 through 10 are the main show in the US and Canada and the trout stands as the fly fisher's standard quarry worldwide. That's why I chose them.

But there are other fishes and other kinds of fly fishing just as worthy of the fly fisher's attention as these. If this were a fly-fishing encyclopedia I'd cover them all; thankfully, it's not—overwhelming detail is the *last* thing you need in order to start out fly fishing. So instead I'll scan just a few more fishes fly-fishers seek.

## FRESHWATER FISHES
### Steelhead and Atlantic Salmon

While there are steelhead and Atlantic salmon that live out their entire lives in fresh water, these fishes are built mainly to migrate out from the rivers and creeks of their birth to oceans and seas, where they feed and grow until spawning draws them back to their home waters. Both fishes are considered members of the trout family by most anglers and, depending on when you ask, biologists.

The steelhead is a rainbow trout with a powerful urge to migrate. It's native to rivers of the west coast of the US and Canada—from as far south as the Mexican Border (although that's the bare end of its range) well up into Alaska. (The introduction of steelhead into the Great Lakes of eastern North America created a fishery that remains strong today, a

century later.) A typical steelhead caught on its spawning run weighs around seven pounds.

The Atlantic salmon is native to the east coast of the US and Canada and to western Europe and Iceland. Average weight on returning to its home river is about 15 pounds.

Steelhead and Atlantic salmon are magnificent fishes long revered by fly-fishers (Atlantic salmon fly fishing goes *way* back). Some fly-fishers spend their lives dedicated to one of these fishes or the other.

### Pacific Salmon

Five species of salmon are native to the west coast of North America, and all but one of these are now established in the Great Lakes. Salmon are definitely *not Atlantic* salmon (confusing, I know) and are also very different from trout, though they look something like trout. Salmon, like trout and Atlantic salmon, spawn in rivers. Unlike trout and steelhead and Atlantic salmon, salmon *always* die after spawning. Salmon spend the bulk of their adult lives in salt water (sometimes standing fresh water...the Great Lakes...), returning to their home streams to spawn. North American salmon species include the silver (or coho), king (or chinook), pink (or humpy), chum (dog), and sockeye. There are other species in other parts of the world.

Usually, salmon are caught in rivers on all sorts of colorful and peculiar flies, which is odd because salmon do not feed in fresh water—who knows why they'll strike some odd fly pattern like the Egg Sucking Leech?

Some fly-fishers pursue salmon not in rivers but along saltwater beaches or even out in the ocean—I've done both, and can tell you that no salmon settling into even the early stages of spawning can match the wild vigor of one in its saltwater feeding prime.

Steelhead

Salmon

## OTHER PANFISHES

The bluegill we explored in chapter 8 really is the king of American panfishes, but there are other panfishes worth pursuing, each with its own unique character.

Black crappie

Rock bass

Neither the white crappie nor the black crappie has ever impressed me with its cunning, but both fight well and gather in swarms for spawning which can make for fast fishing action. The rock bass likes clear water and rocks, rather than mud or waterplants. In contrast to most panfishes, the black-banded yellow perch feeds best in sunshine and can thrive where salt and fresh water mix. Then there are the redear sunfish, green sunfish, pumpkinseed, and more. Every state but Alaska and every Canadian province holds panfishes.

## ODD BUT INTRIGUING FRESHWATER FISHES

When I was a boy in the 1960s not a single fly fisher seemed to consider carp or northern pike worthy of a thought. It's now clear that they were wrong. Today the common carp is stalked on mudflats like an exotic bonefish (which we'll investigate soon) and the toothy pike's assault on a fly is now almost legendary.

The American shad migrates in schools up its home rivers on both coasts of North America to spawn, and fights hard and fast and leaps from the water.

That's an overview of the main freshwater fishes for today's fly fisher. There are others less common that take a fly.

Common carp

## SALTWATER FISHES

Talk about saltwater fly fishing typically refers to *tropical* salt waters—for most of us, this is truly at the exotic end of the fly-fishing spectrum.

The word on tropical saltwater fishes is that most species fight like demons, making the runs and sometimes the aerobatics of a wild rainbow trout seem...tame. Here are some of the tropical saltwater fishes fly-fishers typically seek.

Bonefish

BRIAN O'KEEFE

The bonefish averages three or four pounds, picks and feeds its way over shallow flats, spooks at a roughly presented fly, and seems to run forever when hooked. The tarpon can be enormous—weighing as much as a man—and as mighty and wild-leaping as any fish. The barracuda is a substantial predator who can fly from the water and tear line from the reel and must be handled with care and knowledge since he can take a finger or worse with his mouthful of sharp teeth. The snook is a middleweight fighter loved by many for his cautious feeding—he offers a fine challenge to the fly fisher's skill.

In cold salt waters, fly-fishers seek the striped bass and bluefish, both hard fighters and willing takers of the fly, and Pacific salmon and a variety of less-angler-tormented fishes.

That's hardly the whole list. There are plenty of other varied and magnificent saltwater fishes you can tease into taking a fly.

Tarpon

BRIAN O'KEEFE

# CHAPTER 13

# Tying Flies

Even better than catching a fish on a fly is catching a fish on a fly you've tied. While that's the best reason to tie your flies, there are other very good ones. Here are a few: you can tie any fly dressing you want instead of choosing from the limited selections in the bins of a fly shop or the pages of a catalog; you can tie your flies just as you want them, heavier lighter, fuller, thinner, bigger, smaller...; you can get the flies you need right now (or, at least, as soon as you've tied them)—no waiting for the postman or running out to your local fly shop to find your favorite fly out of stock.

You can learn to tie many simple and deadly fly dressings with just a modest investment in time and effort. Such standbys as the Gold Ribbed Hare's Ear nymph and Clouser Minnow streamer and Sparkle Dun dry fly are all pretty mild challenges at the tying vise.

But a few pages in a general fly-fishing book, a book that also covers casting and wading and selecting tackle and more, won't provide you much of a start in fly tying—and I say this after writing and publishing ten books and a couple of hundred magazine articles on tying flies. So if you want to try your hand at tying, I can recommend three books I just happened to have written: *Fly Tying Made Clear and Simple* or, if you want to start smaller, a little booklet titled *Concise Handbook of Fly Tying*, and for even a smaller start, *Learn to Tie Flies*. Certainly these aren't your only good choices, but oddly, they stand out in my mind...

Note that I haven't suggested that tying your own flies will save you money. That's because for most tiers, it doesn't. Yes, we can tie a fly for, at most, half the cost of buying it, maybe only a third or a fourth. And the tools should pay for themselves in just a few years, perhaps sooner, right? Probably not—we end up tying all sorts of flies we don't truly need, and that eats up the money we saved. We just can't resist taking a swing at all those colorful and innovative and varied fly designs. So we do get something invaluable for our money: the joy of tying a fascinating variety of flies and broadening our skills at the vise (and, of course, those other advantages I mentioned).

But if you really can limit yourself to tying a modest number of perfectly effective fly dressings in only a practical range of sizes, you actually can save money. Good luck—I'd go mad if I tried it.

Fly tying is optional—there are many excellent fly-fishers who don't tie. For me, though, impossible.

# CHAPTER 14

# Safety

Safety should be an essential element of any sport—baseball, skiing, volleyball, archery...—and, for that matter, traveling abroad, cleaning roof gutters, and crossing the street. Let's prepare you to *safely* go out and catch some fish.

### GLASSES

Whenever you cast a fly, you send its hook sailing again and again past your eyes. So wear glasses—clear or dark and polarized, prescription or non—whenever you cast a fly or are even *around* anyone casting a fly. Fly-hooks and eyes...bad combination.

### INSTINCTS

Your instincts may be your best insurance for safe fishing. They're the same instincts that alert a bird to a stalking cat and give a cat the jitters when a coyote is near and warn a coyote not to walk the edge of a crumbling bluff. The bird, the cat, and the coyote learn early in life to *trust* their instincts—trust yours.

If you shudder as you scan the water you're about to wade, don't wade it. In our human world of facts and philosophy and "enlightenment" we often disregard our instincts, but your instincts, combined with common sense, could save your life.

### BARBS

Crushing down the barbs on your fly hooks will protect the fish you want to release unharmed, and will cause a lot less carnage when you hook yourself—and fly-fishers *do* hook themselves. The safest hooks are the sort that doesn't have a barb to begin with, which back smoothly out of a puncture. Unfortunately, commercially tied flies are seldom, if ever, tied on barbless hooks (one more fine reason for tying your own flies).

### COMPANIONS

It just makes sense to go fishing with a friend or two. Suppose you break your leg a mile upriver and no one's around? I could probably come up with another 50 scenarios in which a fishing partner could make your fishing safer, but you get the idea. A friend who stays within sight could be a lifesaver. And a fine fishing companion.

If you do fish alone, I urge you to fish water comfortable to wade or to handle in a boat, near other fly-fishers.

### WADING BELT

Contemporary breathable waders are loose and bulky, which gives you the freedom to step over a log without straining a seam or tearing it altogether. But if you fall into a swift river, such waders will billow and catch the current—and haul you along to where you may not want to go. A wading belt (made specifically for waders) around your waders and waist gathers in the fabric so you can move or swim if you should need to.

### FISH POKES AND BITES

Many fishes (both largemouth and smallmouth bass and bluegills, among many others) have spines which can stab you—such a stab hurts, and could become infected. Some fishes have long sharp teeth and some of those look to use them on whoever messes with them—intentionally or unintentionally, any fish with real teeth can give you a serious bite. Learn about the fishes you seek and handle—or shouldn't handle—so you can do whatever's safe and appropriate.

### THINGS THAT GO BUMP

Know your water—and the creatures that live in it. I've heard of Northerners kicking blissfully about in float tubes in Southern cottonmouth and alligator water—terrible idea! If you wade or fish from a boat, or whatever, be sure you're safe from the things that live in that water.

### FIRST-AID KIT

Keep one nearby, in your vest or in the car or the boat.

### GENERAL

Again—trust your instincts, and don't push yourself or your luck. Knowing the water you fish and the fish you seek can only help you make wise decisions and complete each fishing day healthy and whole.

# CHAPTER 15

# Skip's Tips
A few critical points, some new, some just worth repeating.

1. Do a little research (at the local fly shop, online, through a fly-fishing club, with a fishing guidebook...) so that you can start out on manageable water with manageable fish. Some waters and their fish are very challenging—they're really for seasoned fly-fishers—and will probably only frustrate you. Don't fear tough water—the challenge can be fascinating and you can learn a lot—just don't start with it.

2. False casting is pretty and, when it's working well, pleasing—but it doesn't catch fish. Use only as many false casts as required (which may be none, just a back cast and then one forward cast), to keep the fly in the water with the fish as much of the time as possible.

3. Every time you cut off a fly—and some kinds of fishing require a lot of fly changes—you shorten your tippet. So pay attention and replace your tippet when it gets too short to do its job (that is, allow a dry fly to drift freely, allow a nymph to sink quickly enough, keep the thick part of the tapered leader far enough away from wary fish...).

4. The connection between line and leader can be a problem when you land a fish—that connection tends to resist entering the tip-guide, and once it does it doesn't want to go back out of it. So land your fish with the line-leader connection just outside the tip-guide. This may require some high reaching with your rod.

5. Most fish are lost because 1. a knot fails (solution: tie your knots well and test them with firm pulls), 2. the tippet breaks (solution: set the reel's drag correctly, don't palm the reel's rim so tightly, or use a heavier tippet), 3. the fish is played too lightly (solution: play the fish harder, putting a good, constant bend in the tip-half of the rod), or 4. slack was allowed in the line (solution: with the exception of a jumping fish, maintain *constant* pressure—even a split second's slack may let the fly fall out).

6. Insect hatches often confound beginning fly-fishers. There are the trout (hatches are usually about trout) feeding away on *something*, but on *what*? Don't fret—you don't have to be an entomologist to succeed with hatches. First: watch. You may eventually recognize which insect the trout are taking, and determine how that insect is behaving (drifting freely, scrambling, twitching...). Second: try to catch one of the insects. Third: find a fly that's about the same size and shape and overall darkness or lightness as the insect. And fourth: try to put your fly in front of a fish while making the fly behave like the insect.

7. Fish know when you're distracted (at least it sure seems that way)—check your watch or turn to see what bird just chirped and that'll be the moment your strike indicator goes down or a bass takes your hair bug. Always assume the action will come when you glance away, and then don't glance away.

8. When a tapered leader has had its tippet trimmed off too many times and has become too short, many fly-fishers simply build its length back with a section or two of tippet material. The sections can be 1 1/2 to three feet long. Just try to make the section or sections step down in diameter gradually from the leader to the final tippet—for example, a section of of 3X tippet between the 5X tippet-section and the tapered leader that appears to end at about 1X. This saves the cost of replacing an entire tapered leader.

9. Worth repeating: Never squeeze a fish, even for a moment. When you're holding a trout, let's say, imagine it as a rubber ball that has enough space to roll around just a little, but is otherwise trapped in the cage of your stiffened thumb and fingers.

10. Casting is the first skill a beginner must develop and one he or she must continue to improve upon—new fly-fishers most often fail because they can't get the fly out to the fish. Long casts aren't normally the main point; controlled casts of adequate length normally are. Work on your casting.

11. When I instruct a beginner to let a bass bug lie motionless on the water or not to retrieve a sinking line for a certain period of time, they often draw in line unconsciously, and that's a problem. So, whenever my instructions tell you not to pull on the line—don't, not even a little.

12. When you've had no action for 10 or 15 minutes, 20 at most, change something. Try a different fly, different water, a different technique or depth. If you're catching fish, stay with what you're doing, but if not, change.

13. When it comes to fly movement, doing the right things isn't enough; the *fly* has to do the right things—so watch the fly. If the fly isn't moving but should, make that happen; if the fly is moving and it shouldn't, work that out. (With streamers and some other sunken flies, watch the line—the fly usually does what the line does).

14. Fly-rod ferrules get stuck. Stroking wax onto the male section of a ferrule is good insurance, but no guarantee. When a ferrule does lock up, you and a friend, facing one another, can hold the rod on both sides of the ferrule, and then pull firmly together to pop the stubborn ferrule open. But—*never* pull or push on the rod's guides.

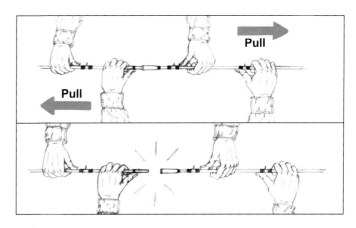

# Index

## A

Atlantic salmon, 75

## B

Backing, 10
Bank, 49
Barracuda, 76
Bass
   fishing, largemouth, 52-57
   fishing, smallmouth, 58-63
   telling smallmouth from
      largemouth, 52
Bass bug, fishing. *See* Flies,
   bass bug, *and see also*
      Popper
Bluefish 76
Bluegill, 52-57
   characteristics, 52-53
   fishing, 52-57
Boats, and other watercraft,
   12
   setting up, 26
Bonefish, 76

## C

Carp, 76
Casting, fly 27-33
   basic cast, 27-30
   feeding line, 30
   mending, 33
   shooting line, 31
   S cast, 32
   versus spin casting, 27
Catch and release, 74
Chironomid fishing, 67
Clothing, 13
Countdown method, 66-67
Courtesy, 74
Crappie, white and black,
   76
Creatures game fishes eat.
   See Feed

## D

Dry fly and emerger fishing
   trout lakes, 67
   trout rivers, 45-46

## E

Eddy, 50, 61
Equipment, 5-14
   caring for, 14
   for largemouth bass and
      bluegill lakes, 53
   list, basic, 14
   for smallmouth bass
      rivers, 59
   for trout lakes, 64
   for trout rivers, 42-43
Experimentation (and open
   mind), 73-74

## F

Feed
   that flies imitate. *See*
      Flies, creatures flies
      imitate
   for trout in lakes, 65-66
   for trout in rivers, 44
Fence riding, 54
Fish
   finding, 34-35
   food for, 34-35
   other than trout, bass,
      and bluegills, 75, 76
   oxygen needs of, 35
   safety, 34
Fish finder 55,
Flies, 11, 15, 18-21
   attractor, 19
   bass bug, 21
   creatures flies imitate,
      15-17
   imitative, 18-19
   for smallmouth bass in
      rivers, 59-60
   for largemouth bass and
      bluegills in lakes, 54
   for trout in lakes, 64-65
   for trout in rivers, 43-44
   tying, 77
   unsnagging, 37
Fly tying, 77
Foam line (scum line), 50

## G

Gadgets and trappings. *See*
   Miscellaneous items

## H

Hand-twist retrieve, 36

## K

Knots, 22-24
   Backing-to-reel, 22
   Blood, 23
   Clinch, improved, and
      Skip's clinch, 24
   Mono loop, 24
   Nail, 23
   Surgeon's, 23
   Tightening and
      trimming, 22

## L

Lake
   reading for largemouth
      bass and bluegills,
      55, 56
   reading for trout, 68-69
   types (pond, reservoir...),
      53
Landing fish, 39-40
   lipping a bass, 40
   netting, 39-40
Leader, fly, 10
   types of, 10
Line, fly, 5-7
   floating, 6
   sinking, 6
   sink-tip, 6
   taper, 7
   weight, 5-6

## M

Miscellaneous items,
   (gadgets and trappings),
   12-13

## N

Nymph fishing
   trout lakes, to rising
      trout in, 67
   trout rivers, 46-47

## O

Observation, 71
Open mind, 73-74

## P

Pacific salmon. *See* Salmon,
   Pacific
Panfishes, types, 52-53, 76
Patience and perseverance,
   74
Perch, yellow, 76
Pike, 76
Playing fish, 38-39
   reel drag and, 38
Pocket water, 49
Pool, 49,
Popper, fishing, 55. *See also*
   Bass bug
Presentation, 72

## R

Reading water. *See* Lake,
   reading for largemouth
   bass and bluegills; Lake,
   reading for trout; River,
   reading for smallmouth
   bass; River, reading for
   trout
Reel, fly, 9-10
   drag, 10, 38
   mounting in reel seat, 25
   options, 10
   parts of, 9
Retrieves. *See* Strip retrieve
   *and* Hand-twist retrieve
Riffle, 48
Rigging up tackle, 25-26
River
   reading, for smallmouth
      bass, 60-62
   reading, for trout, 48-49
   types, 41-42, 58
Rod (fly), 7-9
   action, 8-9
   assembling, 25
   lining, 26
   matching with lines, 7
   materials for, 9
   parts, 7

## Rock bass, 76
Run, 48

## S

Safety, 78
Salmon, Atlantic, 75
Salmon, Pacific, 75, 76
Selectivity, 73
Setting the hook, 37
Shad, 76
Snags, unhooking fly from,
   37
Snook, 76
Skip's Tips, 79
Stealth, 71-72
Steelhead, 75
Streamer fishing
   largemouth bass lakes, 55
   smallmouth bass rivers, 60
   trout rivers, 47-48
Strip retrieve, 36
Striped bass, 76
Sunfishes, redear, green,
   pumpkinseed, 76

## T

Tackle, fly fishing. *See*
   Equipment
Tippet, 10, 11
   types of, 10
Tips, fly-fishing. *See* Skip's
   Tips
Trolling, 66
Trout
   feed for in lakes, 65-66
   feed for in rivers, 44
   fishing in lakes, 64-70
   fishing in rivers, 41-51
   species, 41

## U

Unhooking fish, 40

## W

Waders, 11
   putting on, 26
   types of, 11
Wading, 44-45
Wading shoes, 11